FORM FOLLOWS FUNCTION
THE ART OF THE SUPERCAR

STUART CODLING PHOTOGRAPHY BY **JAMES MANN**

Commentary by **Frank Stephenson**, Design Director, McLaren Automotive

Foreword by **Gordon Murray**, Gordon Murray Design

motorbooks

contents

foreword by Gordon Murray **6**

introduction **7**

4 Ferrari 275GTB/4 **38**

1 Mercedes-Benz 300SL "Gullwing" **10**

5 Lamborghini Miura **48**

Lancia Stratos **80**

9 BMW M1 **90**

2 Aston Martin DB4GT Zagato **20**

6 Alfa Romeo 33 Stradale **60**

10 Ferrari F40 **100**

3 Bizzarrini 5300 GT Strada **30**

7 Ferrari 365GTB/4 "Daytona" **70**

11 Jaguar XJ220 **112**

 12 McLaren F1 **122**

 16 Bugatti Veyron 16.4 **164**

 20 Alfa Romeo 8C Competizione **202**

 13 Ferrari F50 **134**

 17 Pagani Zonda F Roadster **174**

 21 McLaren MP4-12C **212**

Acknowledgments **222**

Index **224**

 14 Porsche Carrera GT **144**

 18 Ferrari 599 GTB Fiorano **184**

 15 Maserati MC12 **154**

 19 Ariel Atom 3 **194**

foreword

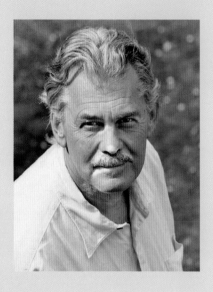

I'm a great believer in the "form follows function" adage when it comes to vehicle design, but there are many different areas that influence sports car and supercar design. Ever since the title "supercar" was first used there has been a debate about the defining elements that transform a sports car into a supercar. Power, speed, and power-to-weight ratio have certainly always been factors, and there have been many discussions around pedigree and history; this subject is probably what polarizes opinion the most. There is also the element of exclusivity—can a high-volume car ever be considered a supercar? The definition will continue to be debated, and it will continue to evolve, with the exception of one part of the equation that has always been there and always will be—design and styling.

I have always been a little outside the conventional engineering "box," as I have been lucky enough to style or lead the styling on nearly all of the 50 or so cars I've designed. I have always loved design and styling in vehicles, whether they be military, racing cars, road cars, aeroplanes, or motorbikes. I once, in a moment of weakness, bought an MV Augusta purely for the design, and I currently have three motorbikes hanging on the wall at home!

Car style is a complex issue; it encompasses size, proportion, highlights, overall shape, and detail design (and that's just the exterior). Proportion is king, whether it's the short nose and long tail of a front-engined sports car or the long nose and chopped tail of a rear mid-engined car, it has to be right—the gateway to greatness.

So is supercar styling art? Absolutely! A sports car is always an emotive purchase, and a supercar even more so. For some supercar owners the art element surely comes first.

During the last five decades, style in supercars has gone through some cultural changes as we have moved from the classic 1960s shapes to the more faceted look of the 1970s, the "not quite sure" of the 1980s, into the mixture of retro, modern, and futuristic of the following two decades. When I was working on the McLaren F1 with Peter Stevens, I knew exactly what I wanted—the proportions, the feel, and the detail. I tried hard not to design a car that could be tied to the 1990s, I wanted a classic proportion and shape that would hopefully never date.

To this day, I have scale models of my favorite pieces of automotive art at home and in the office to remind me to try harder! Amongst my models are the Miura, the Alfa 33 Stradale, the 1960s Lotus Elan, the Ferrari Dino 206 SP, the Porsche 550, and the Austin Healey Frog-eye Sprite.

So, supercars are automotive art, and styling can subtly make or break their future. Not all of them become great cars, and it's probably that intangible that separates a good sports car from a great, iconic car that will keep the discussion going for many a decade to come.

—Professor Gordon Murray

introduction

For many, the phrase "form follows function" is irrevocably tainted because of its association with modern architecture, and some of the brutalist horrors so memorably skewered by Tom Wolfe in his 1981 essay "From Bauhaus to Our House." Not everyone, perhaps, shared this view—not least the architects involved—but even so, what possible application could an aphorism coined to justify an often dour and joyless design philosophy have to the sexy, sensuous, decorative world of the supercar? What can a skyscraper have in common with a Lamborghini?

"I prefer to say form *equals* function," says Frank Stephenson, who kindly agreed to cast an expert eye over the cars gathered for this book. "If it looks right, it *is* right."

Are we perhaps splitting hairs here by substituting the bossy and unequivocal verb *follow* with the more neutral, balanced *equals?* Maybe not.

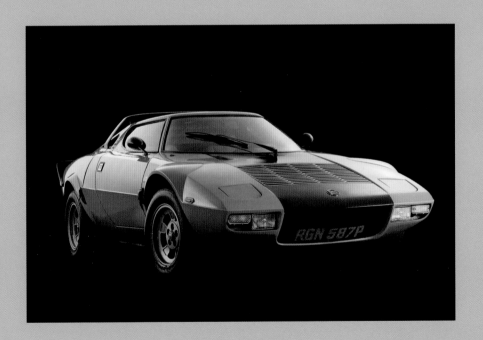

Take another example, the possibly apocryphal tale of Giorgetto Giugiaro's encounter with the Triumph TR7 (not a car that would meet the criteria of this book by any stretch) at the 1975 Geneva show. Having scrutinized the car, with particular reference to the drooping crease along its flank, the co-designer of the Miura reportedly walked to the other side of the car and exclaimed, "They've done it on this side as well!"

Did the creases in question add rigidity to the panels or were they just pointless ornamentation? Would the car have looked better without them or would it still have looked like a bargain bucket knock-off of the Lancia Stratos?

People who write essays on form and function enjoy getting tangled in the semantics, arguing that the use of *follow* means, axiomatically, that function predates form, which surely can't be possible. "Who ever heard of a function existing before form?" they cry.

What a blinkered worldview. The essence of a supercar is not only to perform, but to afford tactile and aesthetic pleasure for the owner and evoke joy and envy among passers-by. That, you may argue, is its function, which surely dictates the form it should take. Even the Ariel Atom (above right), a sports car that is not styled as such, has a beauty of its own: the exposed trellis chassis, welds and all, are redolent of Ducati sportbikes. Here is a car that makes a strong case for not having a bodyshell at all; if you were to be dogmatic, therefore, that form should strictly attach to function, you could argue that the rest of the cars in this book have missed a trick by having body panels. Does bodywork class as ornamentation, and is it therefore, in line with architectural dogma, to be abhorred?

No fan of the supercar could possibly believe that. As Stephenson points out in this book, those people who sculpted the supercars of the pre-CAD era were also artists. They understood proportion, curvature, and surface. The Mercedes 300SL that opens this book may have employed crude (and borderline lethal) swing-axle suspension, but its low bonnet line came about through laying the engine at an angle (first tried, to great effect, in the Mercedes racing cars of the period) and there is barely an inch of wasted metal anywhere on the car. It is a masterpiece of efficiency and one can barely believe that it is half a century old. It lends credence to the belief that the greatest designs are truly timeless.

Other cars in this book clearly belong to an era: The curvature of the 1960s gives over to the wedge shape, followed by a return to the curve. Along the way these cars have changed focus, become racier; while a 1960s Ferrari was a glamorous tool that one would employ either to pose in the street or to swallow continents on a grand tour, a Pagani Zonda combines a cabin fit for a pimp (opposite bottom) with a ride best suited to the track. Supercars have become less compromised and more uncompromising—track day weapons that you would think twice about tackling a twisty mountain pass

in. The limits are too high, the cars (with a few exceptions) too big to fit on most roads. Does that equate to a change in function, or is it simply evolution?

The last car in this book answers the form-function quandary more completely than any other. The McLaren MP4-12C's body shape (below) was dictated by clear-minded engineering virtues: light weight, narrow girth, ideal mass distribution, good visibility, and useful downforce (without producing excess drag). The designers, in effect, imaginatively decorated a shape that had been led by the requirements of aerodynamics, handling agility, and engine cooling. Here, perhaps, we get to the nub of Frank Stephenson's claim that form equals function rather than following it—because if function has indeed led form across the line, it was a photo finish. . .

mercedes-benz
300SL
"gullwing"

1

V ision is the essence of any great supercar; and it was vision that led to the creation of what was arguably the first road-going supercar, the Mercedes-Benz 300SL. To properly put this extraordinary vehicle into context, consider the price when it finally reached production: yours for around $7,000. In comparison, a Jaguar XK140 was a snip at less than half as much.

The early 1950s was an era of austerity in which even Formula 1 machinery was an amalgam of pre-war racing leftovers and fragile hardware pressed into service from production cars. And yet Mercedes-Benz had the vision, in 1951, to return to motor racing and remind the public both of its pre-war racing success and its present sporting credentials. Under the supervision of genius designer Rudolf Uhlenhaut, the first 300SL race car arrived in 1952 and bloodied Jaguar's nose at Le Mans. The production

300SL was first shown to the public at the New York Auto Show in 1954, and the impact was shattering.

The Gullwing, as it became known, was refreshingly clever in many ways but weighed down by compromises in others. Its most immediately unusual features, the gullwing doors, were not an attempt to set styling trends but a powerful example of form following function. Where most cars of the day sat on a simple ladder-frame chassis, the 300SL was underpinned by a rigorously stress-tested space frame. This elegantly welded latticework weighed just 181 pounds, and yet it was far more rigid than a conventional chassis—at a cost of having wide, deep sills below the door aperture. The solution? Find a different way of hanging the doors. Thus the gullwing door was born.

The space frame chassis would also see service in the 300SLR and W196, in which the likes of Juan Manuel Fangio and Stirling Moss dominated the sports car and F1 racing scenes in 1954 and 1955, until the tragic Le Mans accident that prompted Mercedes-

Benz to withdraw from racing once more. The 300SL also shared its engine concept with the race cars. Just one of many compromises enforced by the economic circumstances of the time, the 2,996cc straight six was an all-iron lump, straight from the 300 series sedan. Uhlenhaut's team beefed it up as best they could, first by fitting a torsional damper to the crankshaft so that it could accept the greatly increased horsepower they would liberate by increasing its rotational speed and installing fuel injection. They canted the engine over by 40 degrees to allow a lower and more aerodynamically efficient bonnet line and to lower the center of mass. The result was an output of 240 horsepower at 6,100 rpm, which for the time was an outstanding achievement.

Despite initial fears about the complexity of the fuel injection, the system proved to be reliable and the engine was far less prone to going out of tune than its carbureted rivals. Owners could, if they chose, adjust the mixture strength and idle speed themselves.

During development of the racing cars, it was found that the wide nose aperture demanded by the cooling requirements of the engine and the inboard brakes caused severe aerodynamic buffeting below the hood; a clean, wide exit was required. Thus the production 300SL arrived with dramatic gills on each front wing, behind the wheels. Once again, form was dictated by function.

The other compromises enforced upon Uhlenhaut were rather more troubling. He had to make do with drum brakes from the existing production car parts bin, along with the four-speed synchromesh gearbox. Most onerous of all, though, was the swing-axle rear suspension. Although adequate—and even then only just—for a luxury sedan, in a sports car the swing-axle setup's higher roll center and inherent tendency to change camber were significant hindrances to cornering performance. "Oversteer is apparent, and any easing of the throttle will tend to swing around the rear of the car," wrote *The Autocar* in its typically rigorous road test in March 1955. "It is a car that teaches its lessons sharply and demands respect."

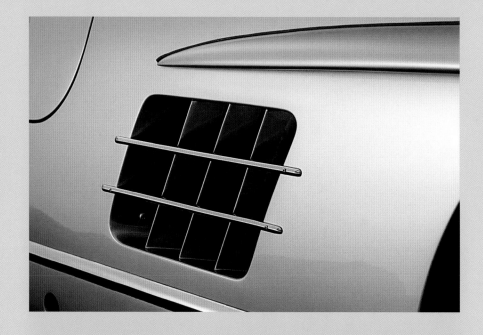

Frank Stephenson

"
This is a sculptor working, almost more than a designer—someone who loves forms, which we all do but back then you had more freedom than you do today. It's a gorgeous car. I wonder if you took those lips off the top of the fenders, whether it would be so interesting to look at? Maybe we're just used to seeing it how it is.
"

Nevertheless, the 300SL combined pace with refinement. It could cruise in comfort at a speed far greater than most other cars on the road. Drivers loved the thoughtful touches, such as the flip-up steering wheel, which eased entry to the beautifully trimmed cabin. The car has gone on to achieve classic status, such that examples now trade for nearly a million dollars each.

It's also important to set the 300SL's handling shortcomings in context. American racer John Fitch finished fifth overall on the ultra-demanding Mille Miglia in 1955 in a 300SL that was almost stock. But for most drivers either its price tag or its temperamental behavior on the limit put it out of reach—or, as *The Autocar*'s road test summed up with almost disdainful hauteur: "The 300SL coupe is available for sale to those fortunate enough to have the ability to handle and the means to purchase such a car. As is well known, these two essentials do not often go together."

Mercedes-Benz 300SL "Gullwing"

Years of production	**1954–1957**
Engine	**3.0-liter inline six**
Output	**240 horsepower at 6,100 rpm**
Torque	**216 lb-ft (293 Nm) at 4,800 rpm**
Curb weight	**2,800 pounds (1,295 kg)**
0–60 mph	**8.8 seconds**
Top speed	**140 miles per hour (225 kph)**
Number produced	**1,400**

aston martin
dB4GT
zagato

2

After several attempts, Aston Martin won the 24 Hours of Le Mans in 1959 thanks to an heroic effort by drivers Roy Salvadori and Paul Frère, the latter of whom would go on to become the *doyen* of motoring journalists as well as a regular sight in the Le Mans pit lane, notebook in hand, for another five decades. But while Aston then decided to withdraw from racing as a factory effort, it still had performance-minded customers who were increasingly tempted by Ferrari's iconic 250 GTO.

The DB4GT Zagato was part of the final flurry of front-engined sports racing machinery of the 1960s, and a contrivance to keep the DB4 going as a racing entity when perhaps it was edging past its sell-by date. The DB4's principal hindrance in

comparison with the competition was its all-up weight and lack of overall torsional
rigidity, a consequence of the chassis construction, which was a simple platform type.
Aston's response was to cut weight out of the body that sat on top of it and to liberate
more power from the engine.

Zagato, the noted Italian coachbuilder, produced a supremely elegant take on
the DB4GT's styling and fashioned it in a series of lightweight aluminum panels that
mounted to the DB4GT chassis via a tubular steel frame. Although the Italian company
traced its history back to 1919, the DB4GT Zagato's flowing lines were the work of
27-year-old Ercole Spada.

The GT chassis itself had a few differences compared with the standard DB4—
no-servo Girling disc brakes instead of power-assisted Dunlops, and the spring rates
and damper settings were different—but otherwise the GT and the Zagato were
very much production-based. That meant wishbone front suspension and a live

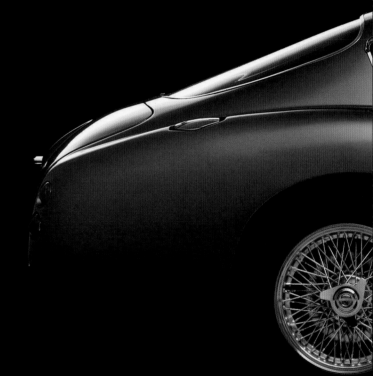

axle at the back located by trailing arms and a Watt's linkage, superintended by Armstrong lever-arm dampers. In comparison, the Ferrari 250GTO had a stiffer shell and its rear suspension was better sprung (with semi-elliptic springs) and damped (via telescopic Konis).

Zagato's bodyshell really did make a difference to the performance, although you could dent its delicate panels almost by looking at them. Perspex windows rather than glass helped shave more weight, which dropped from 2,890 pounds (1,311 kg) to 2,665 pounds (1,209 kg); still rather porky in comparison with the Ferrari. The 3,670cc straight-six engine was treated to a revised lubrication system and a new cylinder head, which retained the twin overhead camshaft but added an extra spark plug to each cylinder, powered by distributors driven by each camshaft. Claimed output was 314 horsepower at 6,000 rpm, although subsequent reports have thrown that claim into doubt; experts now reckon 270 horsepower is closer to the mark.

Even so, the Zagato was a supremely quick and very well-mannered sports car judged in comparison with its production rivals. *Autocar*'s road test in April 1962 praised its comfort and tractability before unveiling the results of the magazine's own performance test: 153 miles per hour maximum speed and 15.5 seconds for the standing quarter-mile. "Mention has been made already of some of the outstanding performance figures, and the rest are best studied by reference to the tables and acceleration curve. They are noticeably superior throughout the range to any others ever recorded in an *Autocar* road test."

On the track, unfortunately, the GTZs that rolled out to face Ferrari had their faces wiped. The 250GTO's rigidity and handling finesse told over the Aston's creamy power delivery when corners were factored in; even the peerless Jim Clark couldn't bring the Aston home ahead of the Ferrari.

Given a straight enough road, the Aston was a match for its Maranello rival once it found its second wind. *Classic & Sports Car* magazine tested a GTZ against a 250SWB

Frank Stephenson

"

This is an incredibly beautiful and sultry design in my opinion, taking the best of British engineering and mating it with Italian flair; what a blend! Although it was more a race car than a road car, it still transmits a feeling of suave sublimity, not the easiest task when combining road and track design characteristics!

"

(and a lightweight Jaguar E-type) at Santa Pod drag strip in 1987 and found the GTZ could clock zero to 60 miles per hour in 6.7 seconds, the same time as the Ferrari; and although the 250 was then quicker to 100, the Aston stormed past to reach 120 miles per hour 2.7 seconds quicker. And while the aforementioned 1962 *Autocar* test had the DBZ reaching a maximum speed of 152 miles per hour, the Ferrari tested by *C&SC* hit the rev limit in top gear at 130 miles per hour.

At £3750, though, the Aston Martin DB4GT Zagato was only ever going to be a limited-run piece of exotica. Ultimately only 19 were built, of which 11 were right-hand drive for the U.K. market. You only have to look at it to see why; besides its undoubted rarity, this car is now one of the most desirable and highly prized classics of all time.

Aston Martin DB4 GT Zagato

Years of production	**1961–1963**
Engine	**3.7-liter inline six**
Output	**314 horsepower at 6,000 rpm (claimed)**
Torque	**278 lb-ft (377 Nm) at 5,400 rpm**
Curb weight	**2,665 pounds (1,209 kg)**
0–60 mph	**6.7 seconds**
Top speed	**153 miles per hour (246 kph)**
Number produced	**19**

bizzarrini
5300GT
strada

3

Giotto Bizzarrini is perhaps one of the unsung engineering heroes of the twentieth century. That his name carries less resonance outside the realm of the car enthusiast is perhaps because his business and political *nous* did not quite match his precocious engineering ability.

Born to wealthy parents in 1926, he attended college at the University of Pisa. After graduation, Bizzarrini initially found work in the chassis design department of Alfa Romeo before his hankering to work on powertrains and to be a test driver led him to Maranello in 1957. It was at Ferrari that Bizzarrini carved out his reputation as a genuine multidisciplinarian, contributing to a number of road and race projects,

of which the 250GTO was his standout achievement: Ferrari's 250 sports car failed to be competitive at Le Mans in 1959 and Enzo put his best engineers, including Bizzarrini, to work on a solution. As well as working on the aerodynamics—by his own admission Bizzarrini was no designer, and the test car was dubbed *Il Mostro*—the key to improving the 250 was to lower the engine (by converting it to dry-sumping) and move it as far back in the body as possible.

Bizzarrini did not have long to enjoy the glory of the resulting car; he and four other key members of the Ferrari organization, including Carlo Chiti and team manager Romolo Tavoni, departed Maranello in 1961 after a furious row involving a forthcoming restructure and the ongoing presence of Enzo's shrewish wife in and around the works. The exiles formed a new équipe, ATS, with the express intention of humbling their former employer on the racetrack, but within months the headstrong Bizzarrini fell out with Chiti over the direction of the project.

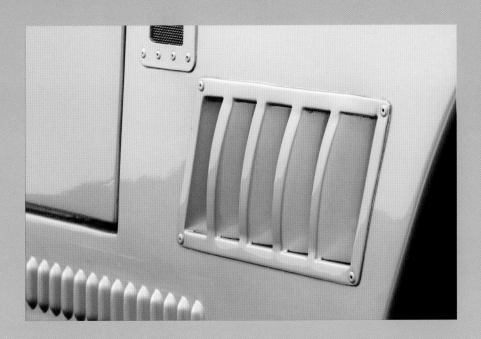

Frank Stephenson

"I've seen a couple of these—the last one was at Goodwood a few years ago. It's funny because they're so much like Ferraris, almost a cousin. For its day it was pretty dramatic—the square wheel cut-outs were interesting—but I don't see it as being as pure as a Ferrari. Still gorgeous, though."

Setting up a freelance consultancy under the name Societa Autostar in 1962, Bizzarrini earned a commission from Ferruccio Lamborghini to design a V-12 engine for the tractor magnate's forthcoming car. But this relationship also ended in rancor when Lamborghini took stock of the finished quad-cam engine, determined that its character was too racy, and dragged his heels over payment.

Salvation arrived in the form of Italian industrialist Renzo Rivolta, who was expanding his Iso empire's reach into the luxury sports car field. Rivolta commissioned Bizzarrini to work on the chassis of the Iso Rivolta, an elegantly proportioned Chevrolet-engined 2+2 coupe. Bizzarrini's feet were not long under the table before he began to lobby for a more race-oriented car.

Development of Iso's next project, the Grifo, proceeded with a shortened version of the Rivolta chassis, and Bizzarrini focused his efforts on a racing version of the car. The differently bodied road and race variants were shown at the 1963 Turin show,

but already fault lines were developing between the consultant and his patron. Rivolta wanted to concentrate on the road-going Grifo A3/L (*Lusso*, meaning "luxury"), while Bizzarrini chased success on the racetrack with the A3/C "Corsa." (racer). Apart from class wins at Le Mans, results were sparse and in 1965 the relationship dissolved. Bizzarrini had a bargaining chip, though: He had registered the Grifo name and negotiated a deal in which Iso got the name and he received enough parts to begin a limited production run of his own. Societa Autostar became Prototipi Bizzarrini, and the engineer became a manufacturer in his own right.

The initial shape of the A3/C, which became the Bizzarrini 5300 GT, was drawn by Piero Vanni and then refined by the young Giorgetto Giugiaro at Bertone. Its layout was determined with weight distribution rather than routine maintenance in mind; the 5.5-liter Chevy V-8 was mounted so far back in the frame that its distributor had to be accessed via a panel under the dashboard. For racers this inconvenience was a small

Frank Stephenson

"
I don't think they're as pretty as other Ferraris of that era. They look as if somebody didn't know where to stop. It's like a mixture of lots of other cars. You can see all sorts of things—a little bit of GTO there, a bit of Jensen Interceptor over there.
"

price to pay for a 48:52 weight distribution. It handled with remarkable poise, and even in street trim it was capable of over 170 miles per hour and zero to 60 in 6.5 seconds.

The car featured in these pages, chassis 0332, has an intriguing history. It was built early in 1965 and used as a development hack throughout the company's short history. Every refinement introduced to the road and race cars was tested on this chassis first, and it remained in Bizzarrini's hands for almost 30 years after the dissolution of his company.

There was an attempt to break the American market with a model featuring independent rear suspension rather than a de Dion tube, but only a handful were sold despite the involvement of U.S. racer John Fitch. Bizzarrini was an engineer rather than a marketeer, and his project ran aground for lack of investment. The company was declared bankrupt after building a few more than 100 cars, and Bizzarrini returned to the realms of consultancy.

Bizzarrini 5300 GT Strada

Years of production	**1965–1969**
Engine	**5.5-liter Chevrolet V-8**
Output	**365 horsepower at 6,500 rpm**
Torque	**344 lb-ft (466 Nm) at 4,000 rpm**
Curb weight	**2,530 pounds (1,150 kg)**
0–60 mph	**6.5 seconds**
Top speed	**170 miles per hour (274 kph)**
Number produced	**139**

ferrari
275GTB/4

t is well documented that Enzo Ferrari only started making road cars to fund his racing activities; and, up until the 1960s, there were very few differences between a Ferrari in which the likes of Olivier Gendebien might take victory in the Targa Florio and a Ferrari in which a well-heeled gent might try to impress a lady around the twisty roads above Monte Carlo. For Enzo, it was a nice little earner.

During the 1960s, though, sports car racing underwent a rapid technological evolution, embracing mid-mounted engines and exotic prototypes. There was still a place for cars that were closely based on their road-going equivalents, but it was no longer at the leading edge. Ferrari's 250GTO and GT SWB (short wheelbase) models epitomized the dual-purpose front-engined sports car; and when the time came to replace them in 1964, the gulf between road car and race car in this segment of Ferrari's range could not be bridged. The race cars would be mid-engined, but Ferrari's road-going flagship would keep its engine in the front, prioritizing stability and feel over fast-twitch responsiveness.

The new 275 Gran Turismo Berlinetta was unveiled at the 1964 Paris motor show. Beneath its classically elegant Ferrari shape, the car embodied a further step change in the company's philosophy. Competition from the likes of Jaguar had persuaded the hitherto mechanically conservative Ferrari to specify fully independent suspension in place of the 250GTO's live-axle rear. Enzo appointed the multi-disciplinarian driver and engineer Michael Parkes—who would go on to drive in six Grands Prix for Ferrari's Formula 1 team—to develop the chassis.

Independent rear suspension was not just a sop to looking good on the spec sheets. Ferrari's engineers had worked on the minutiae, locating the five-speed gearbox (in itself something of a departure for the company, which had previously specified four-speeders

Frank Stephenson

"

This is to die for. Absolutely. I went to a 275 owners' thing once and [1964 F1 World Champion] John Surtees was there driving one. He talked all afternoon. It was amazing.

"

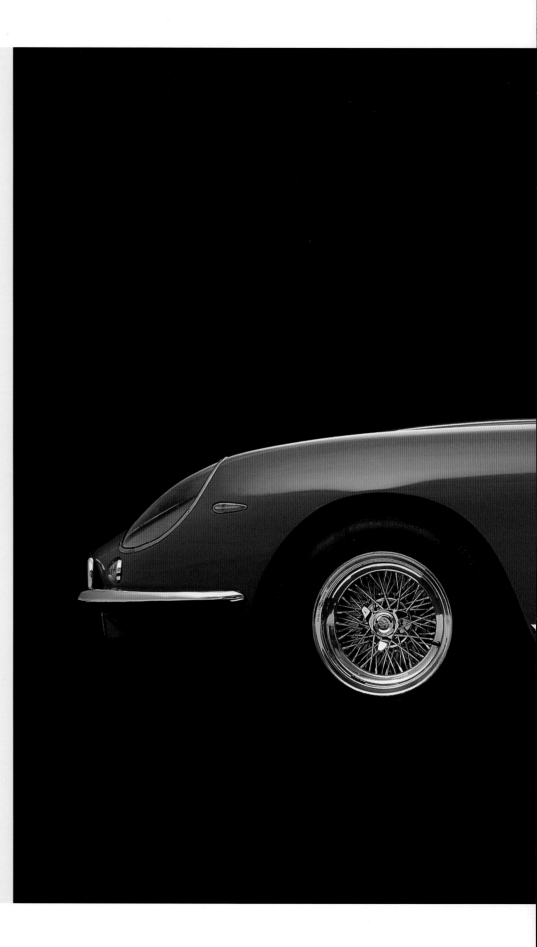

Frank Stephenson

"

This car does it for me. This was when design was just art—functional art, of course—but that could not be anything but a Ferrari. It looks aggressive and sensual; high performance is built in. It's just a classic, beautiful piece of design.

"

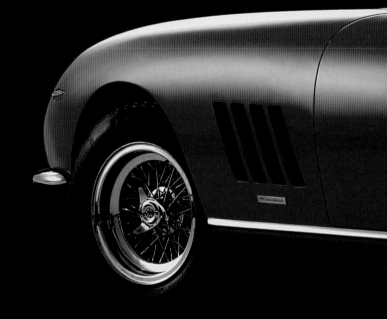

"I didn't love cars like this when I was young, but as I got older I learned more about proportions, simplicity, and beauty. The guys who designed these were artists. Okay, so they didn't have to consider pedestrian impact regulations and things like that, but if you could build cars like these today—you'd sell them all!"

in its road cars) on the transaxle. Combined with a lightweight propshaft, this gave the 275GTB a weight distribution of 49:51, despite the mass of the V-12 up front.

The engine was the classic Gioacchino Colombo 60-degree V-12, now bored out from 2,953cc to 3,285cc. Fed by three Weber carburetors, it delivered a peak of 280 horsepower at 7,600 rpm.

The four-wheel disc brake setup was also a feature that had trickled down from racing, but the constraints of the GTB's 14-inch wheels made for occasionally unpredictable results on early cars. This, coupled with the vibrations emanating from the fragile lightweight propshaft, accounted for the only complaints when the GTB reached the market.

Problems homologating the 250LM race car led Ferrari to produce a handful of aluminum-bodied 275s for racing purposes, and the fruits of that program led to a major update when the 275 was two years into its model cycle. The propshaft, which had

Ferrari 275GTB/4	
Years of production	**1966–1967**
Engine	**3.3-liter DOHC 60-degree V-12**
Output	**300 horsepower at 8,000 rpm**
Torque	**217 lb-ft (295 Nm) at 6,000 rpm**
Curb weight	**2,315 pounds (1,050 kg)**
0–60 mph	**6.0 seconds**
Top speed	**162 miles per hour (260 kph)**
Number produced	**350 (estimated)**

been connected to the chassis by a bearing halfway along, was replaced with a beefier torque tube. The nose was lengthened and re-profiled in order to reduce aerodynamic lift. More importantly, the V-12 gained even more power.

The competition option of six carburetors became standard, along with twin-cam cylinder heads and a dry sump. Peak output went up to 300 horsepower at 8,000 rpm—a modest amount on paper, but on the road the difference manifested itself in better responsiveness and a more aggressive, revvier character.

As a measure of how *de rigueur* it had become to specify vee engines with quad cams, Ferrari renamed its flagship coupe the 275GTB/4. It would prove to be the last Ferrari built on Enzo's watch before the company became part of the Fiat empire; and as such, this beautiful two-seater has come to be regarded by many as the quintessential Ferrari.

lamborghini
MIURA

5

The exact phrasing of the conversation between Enzo Ferrari and Ferruccio Lamborghini that resulted in the birth of another Italian supercar manufacturer has been lost in translation and in the mists of time. But according to Lamborghini himself, his Ferrari had suffered one too many clutch failures for his liking and he resolved to seek out the company proprietor in person in order to make his dissatisfaction plain. Enzo Ferrari, it is said, laughed Lamborghini out of the room: What could a man who made tractors for a living possibly know about supercars?

It's true that Lamborghini made his fortune building agricultural equipment; what he didn't know about supercars—other than as an owner of several—he set about addressing by buying in expertise from elsewhere. He hired the aforementioned Giotto Bizzarrini to design a V-12 engine; aeronautical engineer Giampaolo Dallara and

Frank Stephenson

"

I met some of the people who worked on it. When I was working at BMW, they'd just bought the Rover Group and they wanted to reinterpret the Land Rover—to do an SUV based on Land Rover technology. Dr. [Wolfgang] Reitzle [head of R&D] said, 'I want to see a full-size model in six weeks. That's pretty much impossible, especially in Germany where they don't let you work weekends. So I was asked to go to Turin, sketch the X5, and get it built by a coachbuilder there.

I showed up on a Sunday afternoon with another guy from California and a sketch that I'd just done on the flight, and we went to the studio. It was like a hole in the wall. There were three old guys there, all pushing 70. The translator introduced us, and I asked him if these guys were going to be able to work 16 to 18 hours a day, seven days a week for six weeks. He said, 'Oh, don't you worry, these are the same three guys who modeled the Miura.' I was practically on my knees!

When we'd finished, they gave me the piece they used to model the centerline section of the Miura. It was like a French curve, made of plexiglass, and it was cracked and covered in plaster and varnish, but I had it mounted on a piece of black velvet. It's one of the most precious things I have.

"

Maserati's Bob Wallace came aboard with engineering graduate Paolo Stanzini to work on chassis design. A trip to the Spanish estate of fighting bull breeder Don Eduardo Miura provided both the nascent company's logo and the name for its second car.

Lamborghini's first model—the front-engined 350GT, launched in 1964 and later marketed with an enlarged and reworked V-12 as the 400GT—was priced to compete with Ferrari and sold in moderate numbers. By then Bizzarrini had departed back to the world of freelancing after a dispute over the engineering details of the engine (which Lamborghini felt lacked the necessary refinement), and it was Dallara who enlarged the V-12 from 3.5 liters to 3.9.

During 1965, Dallara, Wallace, and Stanzini made a concerted effort to sell Lamborghini on the idea of a more upmarket, edgier, and racier car. Lamborghini, for whom the initial benchmark for his company was simply to make better and more refined road cars than Ferrari, was not easily sold. But he was interested enough in their innovative mid-engined chassis concept to direct them to build a full-size mockup for the Turin show, his reasoning being that it would position the company as a thought leader—even if he never built a car based on it.

Thus visitors to Turin in 1965 were wowed by a car that didn't even have a body to go on top of it. The box-section chassis was neat and compact, but the highlight was the engine: mounted behind the driver, as it would be in a racing car, and aligned transversely so it remained within the wheelbase. It was enough to have some showgoers reaching for their checkbooks, and Lamborghini almost had no alternative but to go ahead with production.

Bertone won the contract to style the new car, and the matter of whose pen had greatest influence over the final shape has been hotly debated ever since; both Giorgetto Giugiaro and Marcello Gandini have laid claim to its authorship. As Frank Stephenson relates, the work is largely Gandini's.

The styled prototype was ready for the Geneva show at the beginning of 1966 and the first Miura, the LP400, entered production in 1967—beating the Dino (Ferrari's first mid-engined road car) to the market by a year. Its performance was as dramatic

Frank Stephenson

" They said the styling was 95 percent [Marcello] Gandini. Giugiaro was involved at the beginning, but they said that if anybody was responsible for that car it was Marcello Gandini. "

as its appearance: Top speed was around 170 miles per hour, and it reached the European benchmark of 60 miles per hour from a standstill in six seconds. Two series of refinements would follow—The S P400 of 1968, and the SV P400 of 1971 (shown here, one of only seven produced in right-hand drive)—before production ended in 1972 with 764 examples built.

Although its acceleration was staggering and its packaging little short of revolutionary, the Miura presented a challenging ownership proposition. The clamshell construction of the hood and rear deck promised easy access for regular maintenance—and since the mechanical layout dictated that the gearbox share oil with the engine's sump, regular maintenance was what this car needed. The futuristic cabin was an ergonomic catastrophe; as with many Italian cars, attaining a comfortable distance from the pedals left the driver almost out of reach of the steering wheel—and the steering was so heavy that it demanded substantial leverage. The combined engine/gearbox

Frank Stephenson

"

The Miura is every young designer's dream. How they got it so perfectly proportioned, I don't know. I loved it in the orange. If you did it today it would still be futuristic—nobody does the hood as a clamshell. It's possible, but it has to be on a super-supercar because it's so expensive and not very practical. But it adds to the sense of occasion when you come up to a car like that.

"

made for difficult shifting until the V-12, the transmission, and its associated lubricants had thoroughly warmed through; and, regardless of operating temperature, the process of engaging reverse usually required both hands.

Once at speed, the enthusiast driver—ears ringing with the mechanical din of the V-12 and its conjoined gearbox reciprocating just inches away—would have to exercise circumspection when exploring the Miura's limits. Engineers were a long way from properly exploiting the theoretically near-perfect mid-engined layout, making it easy for an overly keen pilot to sign checks that neither the Miura's chassis nor its standard-fit Pirellis were in a position to honor.

Still, the Miura became a performance car icon, and if its demeanor often resembled that of the creature adorning its badge rather too closely, so much the better. Rarely in the history of supercars can any model claim so authoritatively to be both beauty and beast.

Lamborghini Miura SV P400

Years of production	**1971–1972**
Engine	**4.0-liter DOHC 60-degree V-12**
Output	**385 horsepower at 7,850 rpm**
Torque	**194 lb-ft (400Nm) at 5,750 rpm**
Curb weight	**2,745 pounds (1,245 kg)**
0–60 mph	**6.3 seconds**
Top speed	**186 miles per hour (300 kph)**
Number produced	**150**

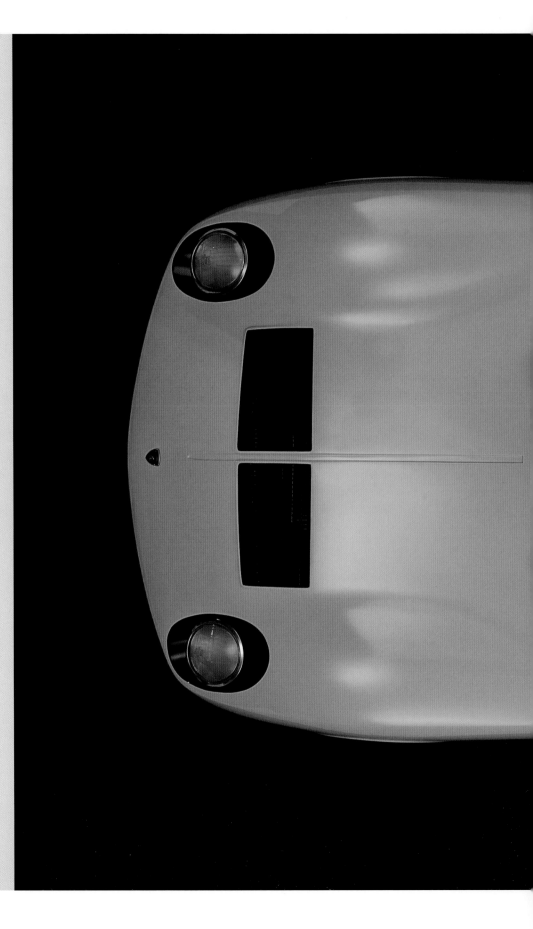

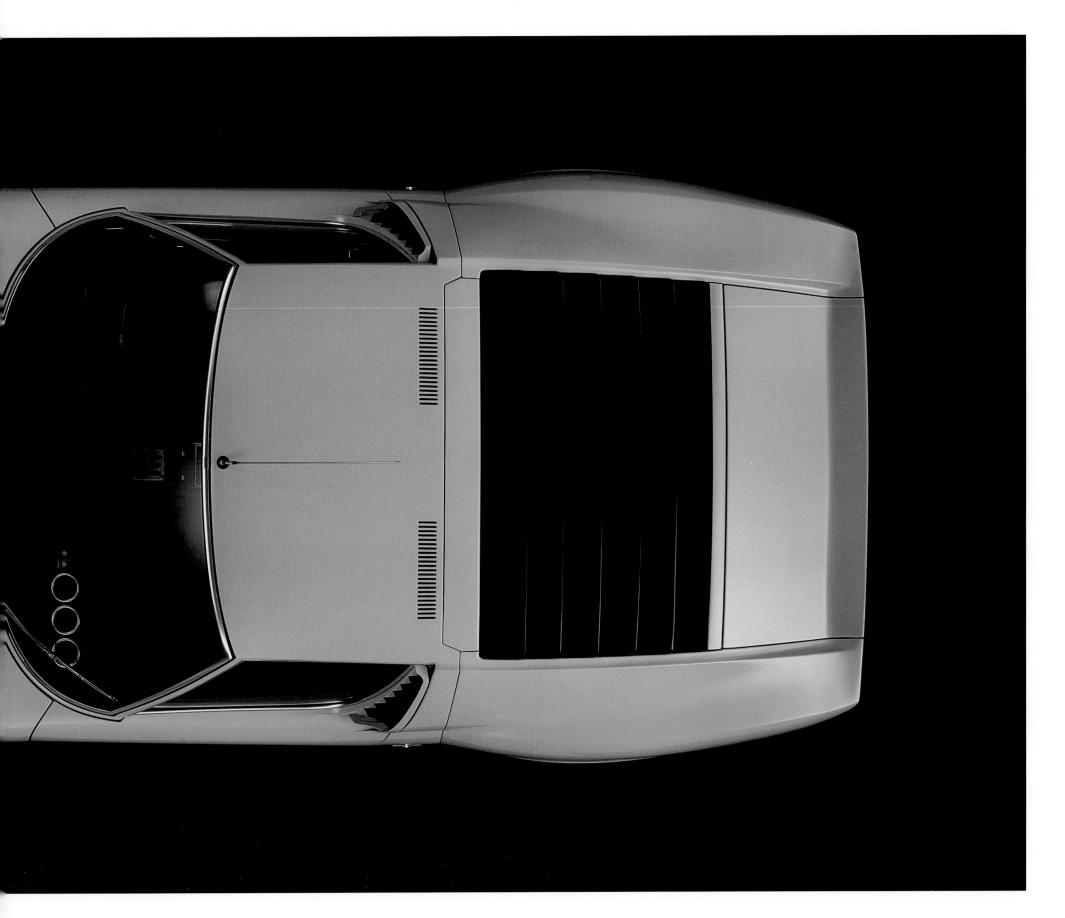

alfa romeo
33
stradale

6

After a decade of licking its wounds following its enforced withdrawal from Formula 1, Alfa Romeo risked economic purgatory once again by returning to motorsport in the early 1960s. Although it would never repeat the highs of its pre-war exploits or its domination of F1 in 1950 and 1951, it would design some legendary sports cars—and in doing so, create one of the rarest supercars ever. According to Alfa's own factory historian, just eight 33 Stradales remain intact and it is impossible to know exactly how many were actually built.

The 33 type number covers a multitude of cars built during the 1960s and 1970s by Alfa tuner Autodelta, under the aegis of the somewhat eccentric Carlo Chiti. Having worked for Alfa's competitions department before moving to Ferrari, then falling out with Enzo Ferrari and co-founding the ill-fated ATS F1 team, Chiti had, in a way, come full circle.

He established Autodelta in 1961 with backing from Alfa dealer Ludovico Chizzola, and in 1963 it was absorbed into Alfa as the company's official competitions arm.

Chiti soon made his presence felt, lobbying for new V-8 and flat-12 engines to replace the small-displacement straight fours Alfa had been using in its GT cars. When the first type 33, a race car, appeared in 1967 it featured a new Chiti-designed 2-liter twin-plug V-8 with fuel injection and an appetite for revs; peak power of 230 horsepower arrived at 8,800 rpm, but it would happily spin up to 10,000.

Frank Stephenson

"

What can I say? This work of art and technology holds the essence of what car designers strive to achieve: functional beauty. It exudes more function and more beauty than any automobile should be allowed to; this car tugs at every emotional string from all viewing angles. To me it represents the epitome of automotive attraction; simple and balanced surfaces that flow together as if created by the forces of nature, with a level of performance that set it above almost all other competitors of its era. This is a design that works so well it would've been a sin to attempt to change it in any way.

"

The chassis, though, was a curious contrivance: two longitudinal alloy tubes with a third transverse tube joining them together ahead of the rear axle. Additional bracing was provided by a magnesium honeycomb at the front, and the bodywork and double-wishbone suspension hung off further magnesium extrusions. The aviation influence was clear (indeed, Aeronautica Sicula was involved in its manufacture), but the design proved troublesome and unreliable. Furthermore, in spite of its light weight, magnesium was rapidly becoming controversial in racing applications because of its predisposition to combust violently in the presence of fire and oxygen. Chiti abandoned the concept in favor of a monocoque.

There is some speculation, therefore, that the road car version of the 33 that wowed the public at the 1967 Monza Sports Car Show was merely an expeditious way of clearing the decks of spare chassis and components to make way for the monocoque

racer. Whatever the truth of the matter, Franco Scaglione's bodyshell for the 33 Stradale was unquestionably his masterpiece. Featuring dihedral doors—which would be adopted by McLaren as a signature design element more than two decades later—the fiberglass body sits on a stretched version of the unloved H-frame chassis. Apparently 18 chassis were allocated to the 33 Stradale production run but only 12 bodies were made; with just those aforementioned eight examples known to exist today.

Although nominally a road car, the 33 Stradale was not so very far removed from its racing cousin. The sparsely trimmed cabin made few allowances for creature comforts, although owners praised the car's surprisingly refined ride; nevertheless the fact that the rev counter dominated the dashboard gave more than a hint that this was a race car, minimally repurposed for the road. When the V-8 was fired up—a complex and inexact operation in itself, given the primitive fuel injection and the extremity of the ignition timing—it would merrily broadcast its ancillary noises through the bulkhead and into the passenger compartment (there is even some anecdotal evidence that it could backfire fiercely enough to blow out the glass separating the engine bay and the cockpit). By all accounts the best method of ensuring a little hush was to go quickly enough to leave the noise behind.

Alfa claimed that it had a block order for fifty 33 Stradales, but if that existed it was never fulfilled. Race car engineering has never, and will never, come cheaply; at $17,000 it was by some margin the most expensive car of its day. After shifting to monocoque construction for the next 33 racer, Chiti would (somewhat inexplicably) revert to a space-frame chassis for what would become the most successful racing variant. Alfa duly clinched the World Championship of Makes in 1975 with the 33TT12, which featured Chiti's flat-12 engine. By that time, the 33 Stradale had faded into semi-obscurity, lovingly maintained by its handful of owners but seldom seen on the road.

If you see one, cherish the moment.

Alfa Romeo 33 Stradale

Years of production	**1967–1969**
Engine	**2.0-liter DOHC V-8**
Output	**230 horsepower at 8,800 rpm**
Torque	**148 lb-ft (200 Nm) at 7,000 rpm**
Curb weight	**1,540 pounds (698 kg)**
0–60 mph	**5.5 seconds**
Top speed	**161 miles per hour (259 kph)**
Number produced	**unknown**

ferrari
365GTB/4
"daytona"

For reasons now obscured by myth and speculation, the car that you and I know as the Ferrari Daytona was never officially given that name. Conceived during the late 1960s as a replacement for the 275GTB/4 and as a further riposte to the upstart Lamborghini, the 365GTB/4 supposedly acquired the Daytona moniker during development, as an internal designation after Ferrari finished 1–2 at the 1967 24 Hours of Daytona. The Ford versus Ferrari battle was an ongoing saga of the sports car racing scene in the 1960s, and all at Ferrari would have been delighted to stick it to Dearborn on Ford's home soil. It's believed that when the Daytona name leaked to the press, Enzo

Frank Stephenson

"Much less voluptuously styled than preceding Ferraris, this slenderly proportioned car is still one of my all-time favorite Ferrari designs. The Daytona is the kind of high speed Grand Tourer that makes comfortable cross-country jaunts one of life's ultimate pleasures."

Ferrari was so furious about the breach of confidentiality that he refused to sanction it as an official model designation.

While the 365GTB/4 did not wow everyone at the 1968 Paris motor show—Lamborghini's dramatically curvaceous Miura made Ferrari's new car look rather *jejune*—in opting for a more chiseled shape, the 365GTB/4 would come to define the look of the 1970s. It would also become one of the most prized classic cars of all time, to the extent that well-preserved examples were selling for a million dollars at the height of the classic car investment boom in the late 1980s. By the same token, though, values then plummeted with the crash—down to around $50,000 in some transactions—and at least one 365GTB/4 ended its life ignominiously, dismembered and buried in the estate of English aristocrat Lord Brockett in an insurance scam.

The 365GTB/4's Pininfarina styling has certainly aged well, particularly the later models with flip-up headlights. Underneath, the tube frame chassis is essentially the

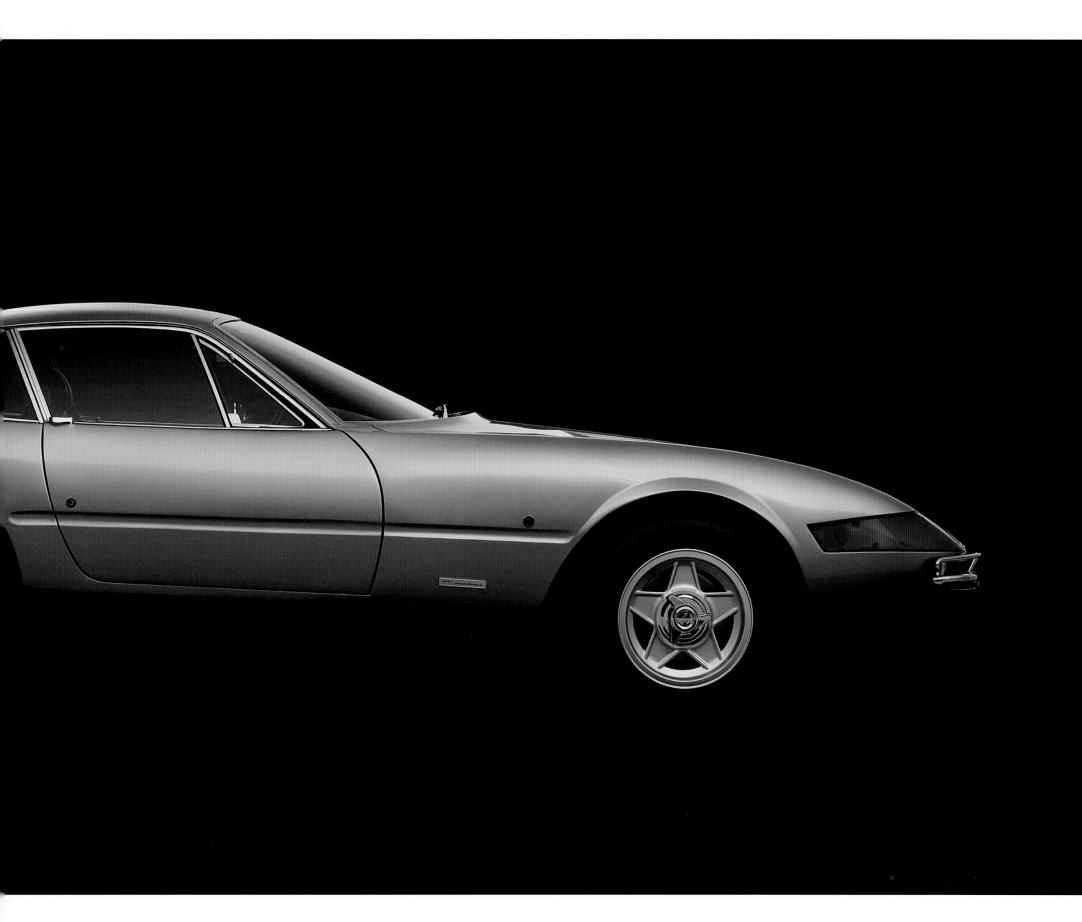

same as that of the 275GTB/4 and the wheelbase is identical, although the track is wider front and rear. Enzo was determined that while his racing cars would be mid-engined (reluctantly, to stay competitive), on his road cars the horse would pull the cart rather than push it. For the 365GTB/4 there would be 352 of those horses, produced by the trusty 4,390cc quad-cam V-12. As with its predecessor, the 365GTB/4 delivered its power through a transaxle, the better to balance its 2,822 pounds (1,280 kg) evenly.

In spite of Ferrari's conservatism, the new car was indisputably the fastest in the world. It was quicker than the Miura across all the performance benchmarks—at 5.4 seconds, 1.3 seconds faster from standstill to 60 miles per hour—and crucially, since the science of engineering a front-engined car was then more advanced than that of the theoretically superior mid-engined car, the 365GTB/4 was more forgiving when the driver broached its limits. "The limit of adhesion is well beyond what is sane and rational on public roads," concluded *Autocar* magazine.

Frank Stephenson

" I much prefer the Berlinetta model over the Spyder because its stunning greenhouse design is integral to the poise of the side profile; it's dynamic and looks ready to sprint elegantly out of the starting blocks. Much of this car's appeal comes also from its successful racing heritage, proving that form really does equal function. "

The unpowered steering was a somewhat ponderous from lock to lock and required substantial effort at low speeds, while the clutch demanded muscle. But this was not a car that was intended to be light and agile, even though Ferrari had used fiberglass in the bulkhead and transmission tunnel to cut weight; rather, it was a car you could slot into a high gear and cover huge distances at interstellar speeds. This was proved beyond doubt when Coco Chinetti, the son of U.S. Ferrari importer Luigi Chinetti, won the Index of Thermal Efficiency at Le Mans in 1971 in a 365GTB/4. The following year 365GTB/4s dominated the GT class, finishing 1–2–3–4–5.

It was not only the fastest car of its time; it would continue to be the fastest car in the world until the mid-1970s. Fittingly, given the great local rivalry, it would be a car from Ferruccio Lamborghini's stable that finally toppled the Ferrari.

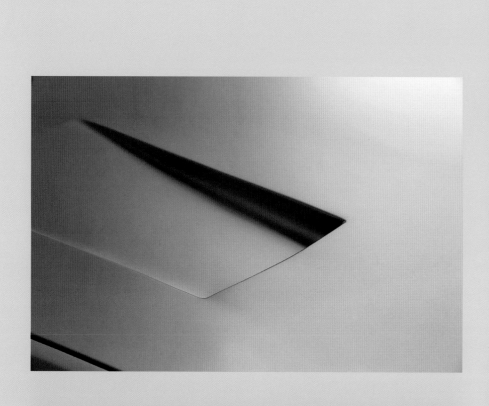

Ferrari 365 GTB/4 "Daytona"

Years of production	**1968–1974**
Engine	**4.4-liter DOHC 60 degree V-12**
Output	**352 horsepower at 7,500 rpm**
Torque	**330 lb-ft (447 Nm) at 5,500 rpm**
Curb weight	**2,822 pounds (1,280 kg)**
0–60 mph	**5.4 seconds**
Top speed	**174 miles per hour (280 kph)**
Number produced	**1,285 (approximately)**

lancia
STRATOS

8

By 1970, Bertone's Marcello Gandini was one of the car design world's hottest properties. That year Lancia unveiled the latest product of his industrious pen at the Turin motor show: The Lancia Stratos Zero was an outrageous piece of styling, and though as a car it was somewhat impractical (entry and egress was achieved via a lift-up flap that included the windscreen), its "cab-forward" proportions preempted mainstream supercar styling by the best part of two decades. Of more immediate note was that its wedgy styling, along with that of Gandini's Lamborghini Countach, would come to define the supercar template for the 1970s.

It was a calling card for a new era at the previously debt-ridden Lancia, which had been snapped up for a token amount by Fiat in 1969.

The concept car was rather too futuristic for mainstream production—although 18 years later it would play a cameo role in the Michael Jackson vanity flick *Moonwalker*—but its compact mid-engined chassis and short wheelbase struck a chord with the competitions department. Work began on a rally car that would ultimately resemble the show star only in its name and its dramatic wedge-like proportions.

Bertone had a prototype ready for the 1971 Turin show, albeit with a Ferrari Dino V-6 shoehorned in the rear in place of Lancia's own putative racing engine, which was not ready. Though still dramatic and aggressive, it was far less outlandish than its show car progenitor; in fact it looked rather like a shrunken Lamborghini Miura. Under the supervision of Miura engineer Giampaolo Dallara, the charismatic Cesare Fiorio, and former Ferrari F1 driver Michael Parkes (a gifted engineer whose Grand Prix driving career had been brought to an early conclusion by a 150-mile-per-hour crash at the 1967 Belgian GP), development progressed throughout 1972 and 1973. Double Italian

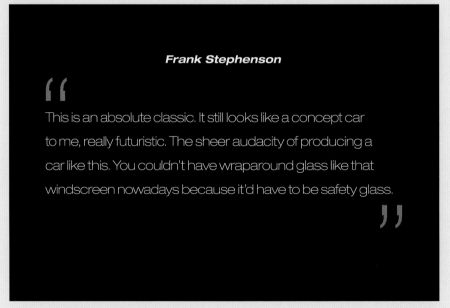

Frank Stephenson

"

This is an absolute classic. It still looks like a concept car to me, really futuristic. The sheer audacity of producing a car like this. You couldn't have wraparound glass like that windscreen nowadays because it'd have to be safety glass.

"

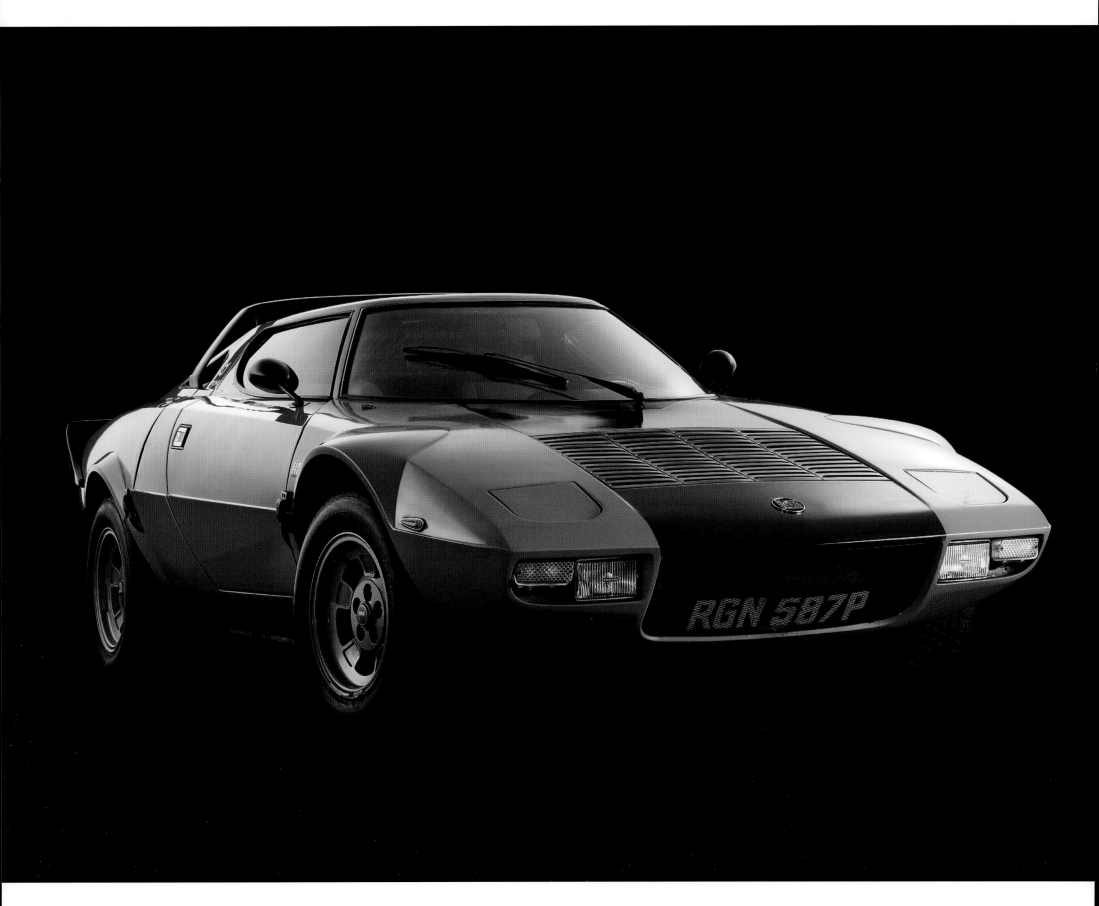

Rally Champion Sandro Munari entered several rallies that permitted prototypes, but this could only be a toe-in-the-water exercise until sufficient road-going examples were built to ensure homologation.

Munari won two rallies in 1973 powered by the 2,418cc 65-degree V-6 Dino. By then the necessary deals had been closed behind the scenes within the upper echelons of the Fiat empire to press on with production of the Stratos with Dino power. Ferrari was replacing the Dino anyway, and shifting the spares inventory was a neat way of benefiting from the internal money-go-round.

Fewer than 500 examples of the Stratos would ultimately be built, but by the time former Le Mans winner Paul Frère had visited the factory and signed off its homologation on October 1, 1974, Lancia's monster was well on its way to winning its first World Rally Championship. It would win the manufacturers' title again in 1975 and 1976 (there was no drivers' championship at the time), taking 17 WRC victories before a rationalization

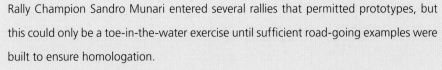

Frank Stephenson

" For me, the proportions are spot on. It touches the nerve that all cars like this should—it gives you goose bumps. You can imagine getting inside it and looking out and thinking, 'Wow—I'm in a Stratos.' It wouldn't be comfortable, because they weren't designed ergonomically. You'd never be able to make a car like this today—they'd shoot you when they saw the first sketches. It's dramatic and beautiful. "

of the Fiat group's racing activities brought the works program to a conclusion. The Stratos would see action in private hands until well into the 1980s.

Although the road car's output was capped at 190 horsepower, development of a new four-valve head brought the rally car to 240; the addition of a turbocharger yielded 560 horsepower for the Group 5 variant, but it was never reliable. With the V-6 located not far aft of the driver's head to give a 46:54 weight distribution, the engine's rumble defines the Stratos experience. It is not a car to be trifled with, even in its least powerful incarnation; the short wheelbase gave great agility on the twisting stages of the WRC calendar at the considerable risk of snap oversteer. It was the panache of naturally gifted drivers such as Munari, Björn Waldegård, and Markku Alen that made this car dance, marshaling its every twitch with a corrective flick on the steering (which, at 3.5 turns from lock to lock, was sharp without being hair-trigger).

Today the cabin is the biggest giveaway that the road-going Stratos was low on

Frank Stephenson

"
When you look at these cars as a youth they always seem much bigger; when you get older they look really tiny. This is a small car; you get inside it and you wonder how they made something so tightly packaged be so dramatic.
"

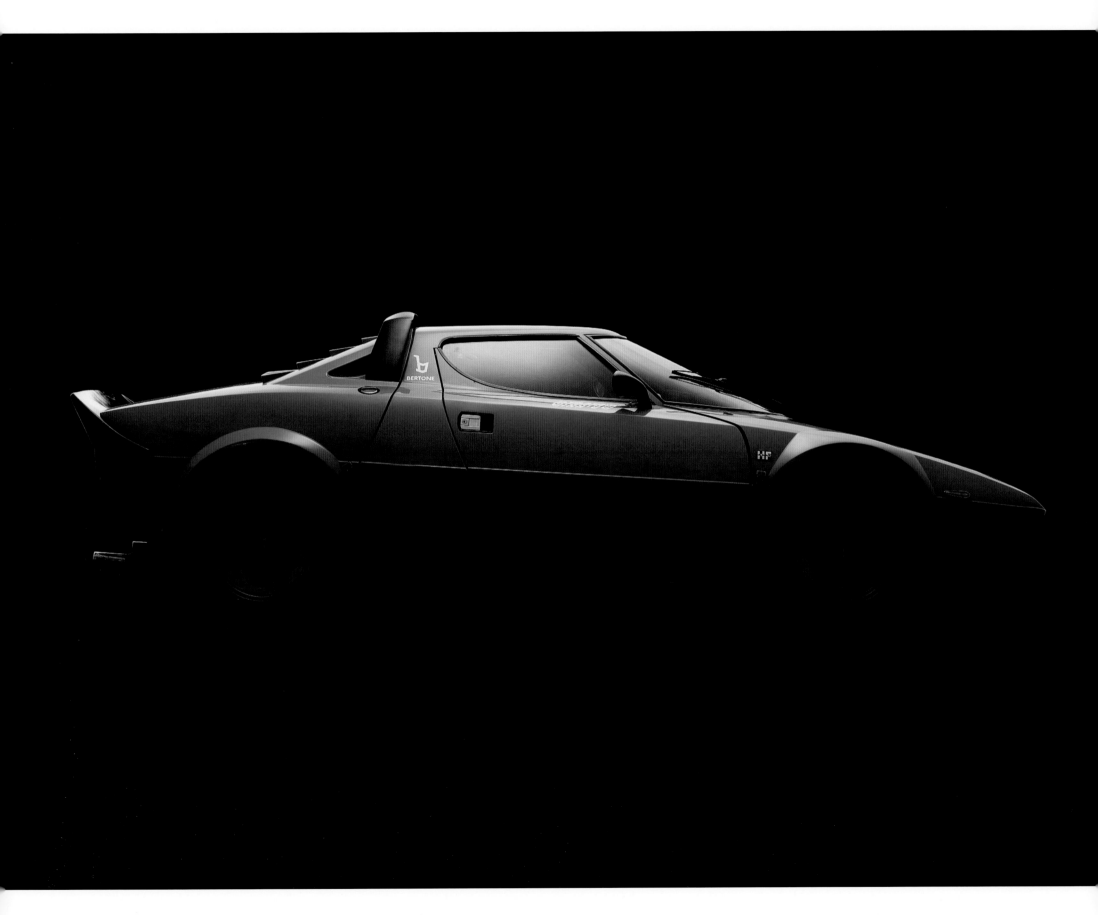

Lancia's priority list: The scattered switchgear is straight out of the parts bin and the upholstery is approximately finished. The windows hinge rather than wind down and are held in place by friction alone. Lancia only obtained type approval to sell the car in a handful of European countries, and demand proved so low that the Stratos remained nominally on sale long after production had actually ended.

But the Stratos was not unloved. Austrian enthusiast Christian Hrabalek has spent the past decade and a half snapping up used examples for his private collection and recently unveiled what may be the ultimate monument to Lancia's icon: a modern reinterpretation of the Stratos, commissioned by Hrabalek himself and designed by Pininfarina, based on the running gear of the Ferrari F430.

To the rallying enthusiast, it will forever define an era when the family saloons that had been the sport's mainstay briefly gave way to stylish exotica.

Lancia Stratos HF

Years of production	**1973–1975**
Engine	**2.4-liter Ferrari Dino V-6**
Output	**190 horsepower**
Torque	**166 lb-ft (225 Nm) at 5,500 rpm**
Curb weight	**2,161 pounds (982 kg)**
0–60 mph	**6.8 seconds**
Top speed	**143 miles per hour (230 kph)**
Number produced	**500 (including prototypes)**

bmw
M1

9

The notion of a BMW, with all the thoroughly defined Teutonic design cues that entails, wearing a crisp Italian suit may seem outlandish—but for a brief, startling moment in the late 1970s it came to pass. The M1 marks an important point in BMW's transition from a provincial manufacturer of quirky, cheap "bubble cars" to a powerful and internationally recognized driver-focused brand.

BMW had been working on its sporting credentials throughout the 1970s, initially with a lightweight version of the 3.0 CS sedan in touring car racing. By 1975 it was active in the American International Motor Sports Association (IMSA) series, and when the Federation Internationale de l'Automobile (FIA) reclassified the categories in sports

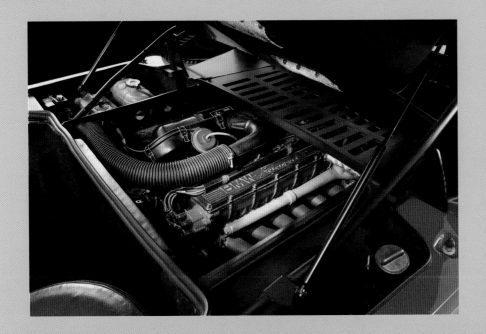

car racing for 1976, an opportunity presented itself. Group 5, which had hitherto been the domain of exotic two-seater prototypes, became a category for heavily modified "special production cars." The rules stipulated that the silhouette of the race car—various hard points including the hood, roof, doors, and trunk—and the location of the engine had to be the same as the production car, but apart from that it was very close to an open book.

BMW gave Porsche a scare in the World Championship of Makes that year, scoring 85 points to Porsche's 95, with the nearest competitor (Ford) back in third with just 8 points. The only obstacle to future growth was the square-rigged, front-engined CSL itself; BMW's competitions director Jochen Neerpasch realized that a wedgier mid-engined car would make a better base. It would be designed as a racer from the off, then retrospectively re-engineered into a road car to satisfy the homologation requirements.

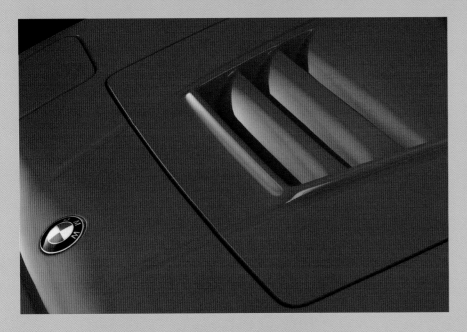

Frank Stephenson

I remember this car—it was one of three I fell in love with when I was a kid, the others being the Ferrari Dino and the Mercedes C111. I used to go to the library and check out *Road & Track* magazines. I'd have cut the pages out if I could! Those were the kind of cars that made you tingle. Then this came out and I thought, 'Wow, BMW does it too!'

So far so good. However, BMW believed it lacked the production capacity and the necessary expertise to build a low-volume supercar. It would have to outsource. It would also have to build 400 examples of the road car before it became eligible for racing.

The answer lay south in Sant' Agata, where Lamborghini was struggling to make ends meet. The M1 would be built alongside the Countach, and its space-frame chassis—also designed by Lamborghini—would be clothed in a fiberglass body styled by Giorgetto Giugiaro's Ital Design. Beating at the heart of it would be BMW's trusty iron-block 3.5-liter straight-six engine, hopped up with a light alloy twin-cam head and driving the wheels through a five-speed ZF gearbox. In road trim the engine was good for 277 horsepower at 6,500 rpm; the race version was heavily modified, with different cam drives and throttles, to give 470 horsepower at 9,000 rpm. It was to be a financially advantageous project for all concerned.

> ### *Frank Stephenson*
>
> And yet it doesn't really look like a BMW. You have the old-style kidney grille and a little bit of a Hofmeister kink, but it's not very Germanic. I loved the car for itself, even though it didn't have the family look. I think I preferred the rear view of it; back then, splitting the body like that [with an indented black line around the waist] was very Italian. It made the body seem a lot lighter. They don't do that anymore—you can do other things to the metal to make it look lighter.

Only it wasn't. Lamborghini's parlous financial circumstances quickly brought the project to a halt; the company could not obtain credit to acquire sufficient parts inventory to fulfill the production run. By 1978, it was insolvent and only a scant few M1s had been built. The Stuttgart-based coachbuilder Baur took over final assembly, but there were still not enough M1s to make homologation. Neerpasch's next move would be a PR masterstroke, although it would not ultimately rescue the M1 project from being a financial disaster for BMW.

Rather than plow on with homologating the M1 for an existing series, Neerpasch created his own—and, working with Max Mosley and Bernie Ecclestone, then leading lights of the Formula One Constructors Association, he placed it in the most public place possible. The Procar championship was a one-make series for M1s that ran on the support card of European F1 races in 1979 and 1980, and as a bonus the top five qualifying drivers in the F1 race each weekend could also enter the Procar shootout and

Frank Stephenson

"
It's like a spacious supercar—you can see the cabin is a decent size. And the pop-up headlights? Wow! They seemed very futuristic. Although I don't think there's any car with them that actually looks better with them up.
"

be paid well for so doing. Sponsorship conflicts ruled some F1 drivers out, but Procar still attracted the likes of Niki Lauda, Alan Jones, Clay Regazzoni, and Nelson Piquet.

Although some of the racing M1s were built by Osella in Italy, the majority were made by the U.K.-based Formula 2 outfit Project Four. For some, then, the M1 genuinely was a financially advantageous project.

BMW's interest in the costly Procar effort fizzled out once M1 production crossed the magic 400 mark. The cars were sold to privateers, many of whom raced successfully for years to come, while BMW focused on its F1 engine program. In 1980, Project Four merged with the struggling McLaren F1 team at the behest of their mutual sponsor, Marlboro, and the operation came under the control of Project Four boss Ron Dennis; a decade later McLaren would use BMW power for its own supercar. Nelson Piquet, driving one of Ecclestone's Brabham cars with BMW's outrageous turbocharged four-cylinder engine, won the F1 world championship in 1983.

But BMW has yet to make another supercar.

BMW M1	
Years of production	**1978–1981**
Engine	**3.5-liter DOHC inline six, 24 valves**
Output	**277 horsepower at 6,500 rpm**
Torque	**243 ft-lbs (330 Nm) at 5,000 rpm**
Curb weight	**2,866 pounds (1,300 kg)**
0–62 mph/0–100 kph	**6.5 seconds**
Top speed	**155 mph (250 kph)**
Number produced	**400**

ferrari
F40

10

How best to celebrate four decades of building some of the most desirable road cars and successful racing cars in the world? To Enzo Ferrari it was a no-brainer: build a car.

The F40 was neither big nor especially clever—certainly in comparison with the techno-showcase that was Porsche's 959—but in its devastating simplicity it was a calculated reminder to the men in Stuttgart that while they had but one Formula 1 victory to their name, Scuderia Ferrari was (at the time) closing in on 100.

When it arrived in 1987, the F40 laid claim to being the fastest car in the world, capable of hitting 201 miles per hour all out and making the zero-to-60 sprint in 3.7 seconds. The previous incumbent, the 959, topped out at 197 miles per hour.

To fulfill the race-car-for-the-road brief, Pininfarina drew an appropriately taut and purposeful shape. Forward thrust came courtesy of a 2,936cc twin-turbo V-8, an enlarged version of the engine that had first seen service in the 1983 288 GTO, a homologation special developed for the FIA's stillborn Group B racing series. This lump, as well as much of the plumbing for its turbo and ancillaries, was visible through a transparent engine cover that, like the side glazing, was plastic rather than glass.

Where the 959's turbocharged flat six drove all four wheels, the F40 eschewed such weight and complication, transmitting the V-8's power to the rear wheels only via a five-speed manual gearbox. Two years after the F40's launch, Ferrari would introduce the world to semi-automatic shifting in F1.

The chassis was also race-bred, though still relatively basic: a steel space frame with bonded Kevlar inserts. Most of the bodywork was carbon fiber, and the interior was light on creature comforts. Upon entering, you would pull the untrimmed door shut with a simple fabric loop, and if you sought ventilation the window slid open rather than winding down. There was no carpet on the floor, though the dash was covered—

Frank Stephenson

"
I bought three Burago models of this when it first came out. I had no money, but I'd heard that it was going to be the ultimate classic Ferrari so the models would sell out!
"

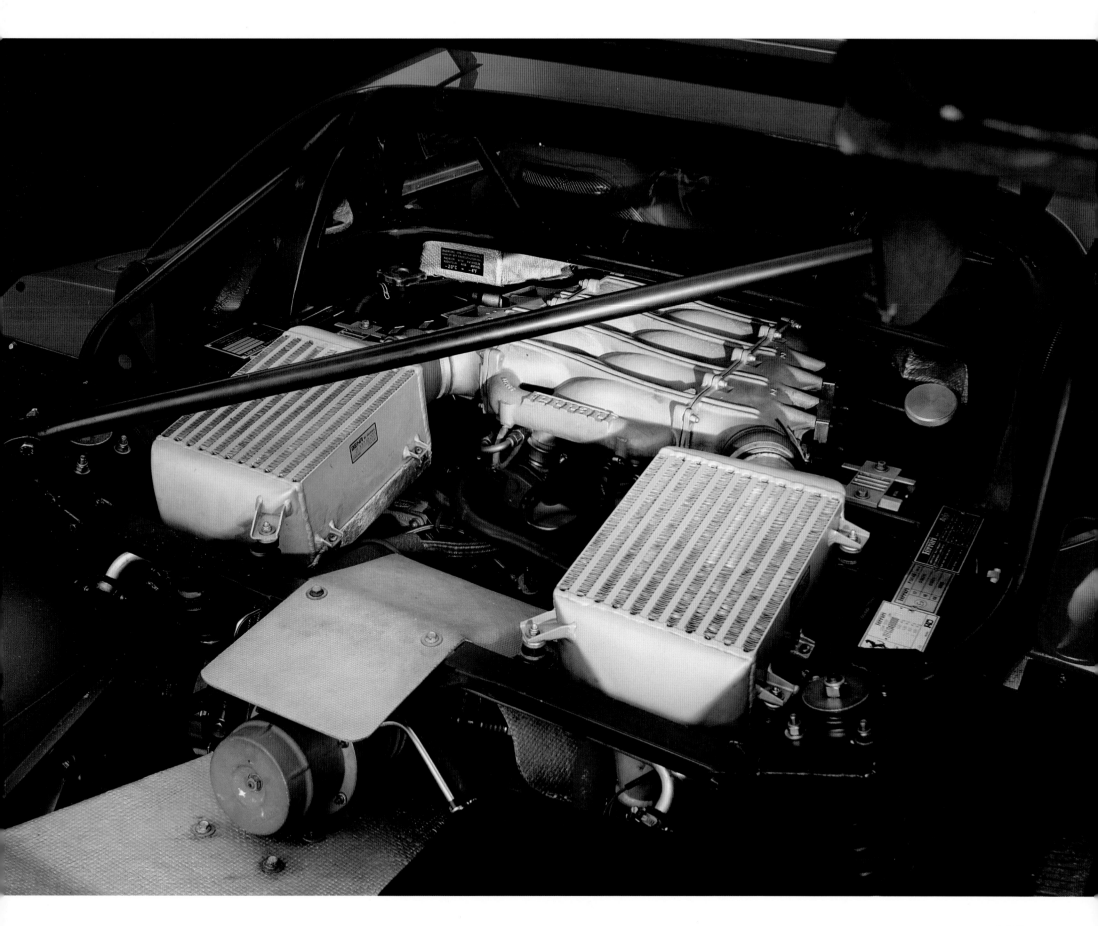

Frank Stephenson

"

It was a big influence when I was involved in the design of the Ford Escort RS Cosworth back in the late 1980s. I pinched the fenders from the F40. The rear wing? No, that came from the Fokker DR1, the Red Baron's World War I fighter plane. I wanted to use the three-wing layout, but the bean counters knocked off the middle one. . . .

"

"trimmed" is perhaps too exacting a word—with a thin fabric that one might expect to find in a warehouse at well under $5 a square foot. The Momo steering wheel fed inputs to the front wheels without the benefit of power assistance. In all, this brought the weight to a racy 2,723 pounds (1,235 kg).

Even without the benefit of turbocharging, the F40 would not have been slow. At full throttle it would romp toward the horizon with gusto, but the real surprise arrived at 4,000 rpm when the blowers came on song. Almost within a blink of an eye the flat-plane V-8 would be howling up to the redline, demanding another gear. Its demeanor was every bit as exciting and dramatic as its appearance.

The F40 was no restful grand tourer but it was an immensely desirable road rocket. Pricing the car at a comparatively modest £193,000, Ferrari rapidly sold the 400 examples it expected to make. Second-hand cars changed hands at well over list price—Ferrari F1 driver Nigel Mansell would sell his for nearly a million pounds—so Ferrari sensibly fulfilled demand by making more: 1,315 in all before production ended in

Frank Stephenson

"

It's very dramatic and it was one of the first real supercars—it's so *raw*. Perspex windows and those vents in the back, no meat over the front wheels—the proportions are absolutely gorgeous. I still love it when I see one today. I look at it in a different light, of course— back then it was cutting edge; now you think, 'Hmmm, it could be a bit more sensual and beautiful.' It was so expensive, but then you got inside and you had to slide the windows open yourself and pull the door shut with a little nylon loop. I think that added to the mystique of it.

"

1992. Later models gained adjustable suspension to improve ground clearance, and—in a somewhat retrograde step—wind-up windows.

Sadly, Enzo Ferrari did not live to appreciate the magnitude of his final triumph against the old foe: He passed away in 1988.

In many ways a car of its time—brash, thrusting, mildly vulgar—the F40 remains an icon. Although its theoretical performance benchmarks have long since been exceeded by the likes of the McLaren F1 and the Bugatti Veyron, the motoring press and wealthy enthusiasts alike can never resist the comparison. Time and again F40s are brought out of retirement to drive back-to-back against the latest, greatest, fastest machinery—and time and again the car proves that magic, plus a dose of Enzo charisma, will endure.

"If you could show me someone who reckons the Ferrari F40 is not the most exciting supercar ever to grace the public road," said veteran *Autocar* road tester Andrew Frankel, "there's a good chance I could show you someone who's not driven one."

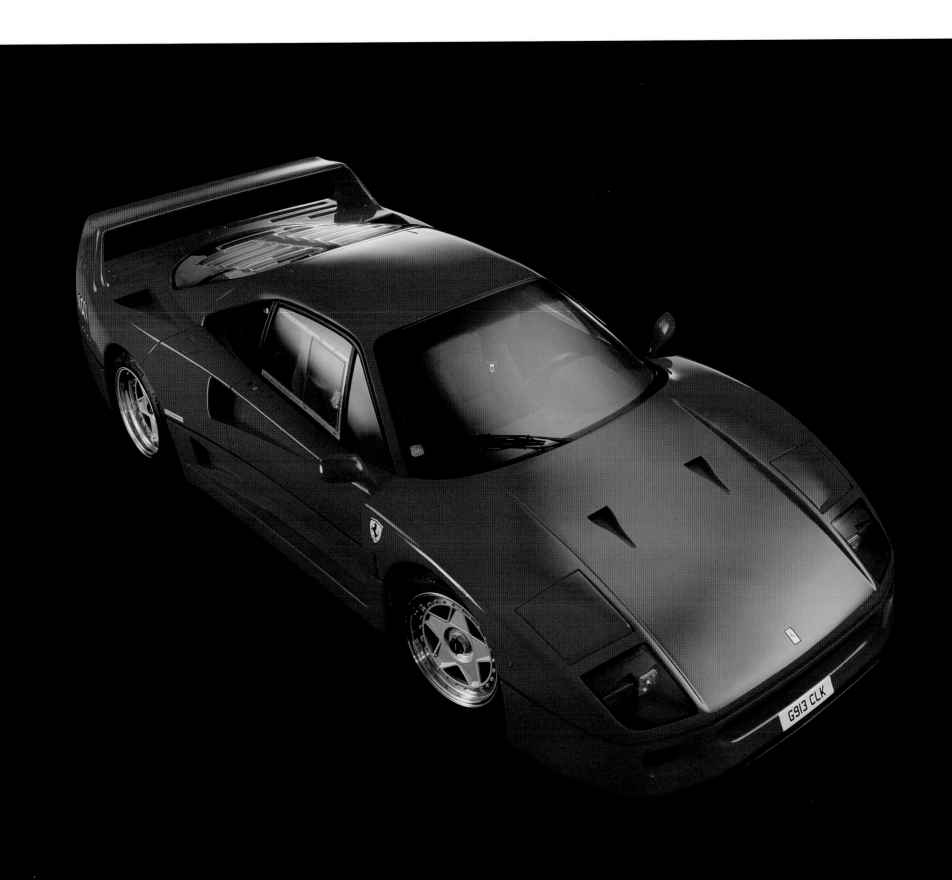

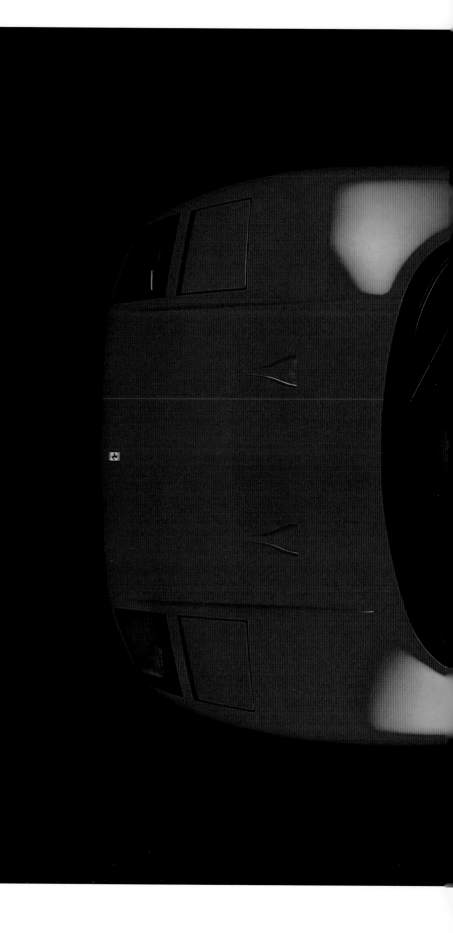

Ferrari F40

Years of production	**1987–1992**
Engine	**3.0-liter twin-turbo 90-degree V-8, 32 valves**
Output	**478 horsepower at 7,000 rpm**
Torque	**423 lb-ft (573 Nm) at 4,000 rpm**
Curb weight	**2,723 pounds (1,235 kg)**
0–60 mph	**3.7 seconds**
Top speed	**201 miles per hour (323 kph)**
Number produced	**1,315**

jaguar
XJ220

11

A well-worn British saying has it that, "There's many a slip twixt cup and lip." In the case of the Jaguar XJ220, a very noticeable "slip" between the initial unveiling of the concept and the eventual appearance of the finished item clouded judgments of what we can now say was an undeniably brilliant car.

In the 1980s, many senior Jaguar engineers met regularly out-of-hours to work on pet projects. The Saturday Club, as it was called, gathered its energies to make something of a sketch by head of engineering Jim Randall: If Jaguar was to make the fastest car in the world, what would it look like?

The British car industry almost died on its feet in the 1970s and early 1980s, and Jaguar had suffered along with it. But in the late 1980s, Jaguar embarked on another push into motorsport—an attempt to recapture the glory days of the 1950s, when it fought with the likes of Mercedes-Benz and Ferrari at Le Mans. Thus the XJ220, deriving its name from its target top speed, was greenlit and became a mainstream project. In 1988—the year a Tom Walkinshaw Racing–built XJR-9 driven by Jan Lammers, Andy Wallace, and Johnny Dumfries broke Porsche's stranglehold to deliver Jaguar's first Le Mans win since 1957—the public got its first glimpse of the XJ220 concept car. It was four-wheel drive, stunning to behold, and, like the XJR-9, powered by a mighty V-12 engine.

The XJ220 would be built in a new facility by Jaguar Sport, a joint venture with TWR. It would cost £360,000. The inevitable slew of car-mad rock stars and celebrities—Elton John, Eric Clapton, Nick Mason, et al.—rushed to lay down deposits of £50,000. Behind them in this veritable conga line of prospective purchasers came a host of ghouls and speculators. For this was the apogee of the greed-is-good era, when a newly launched supercar could be sold on at double or even triple the list price when demand outstripped supply.

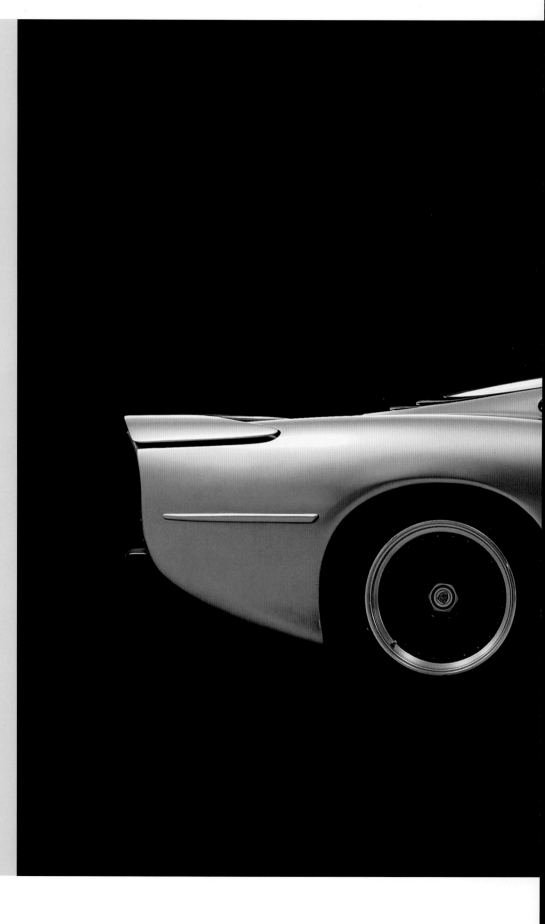

Frank Stephenson

"
This was super-dramatic when it came out. I thought it was the future. And it just looks better all the time for me. It's a massive car—I think that's what gave it a lot of impact when it first came out. Look at the overhang in front; it just goes on forever. The back's the same and the wheelbase is pretty long, too. I love the headlamps—they rotate—and the glass graphic on the side. And it could only be a Jaguar. It's gorgeous and it has real presence.
"

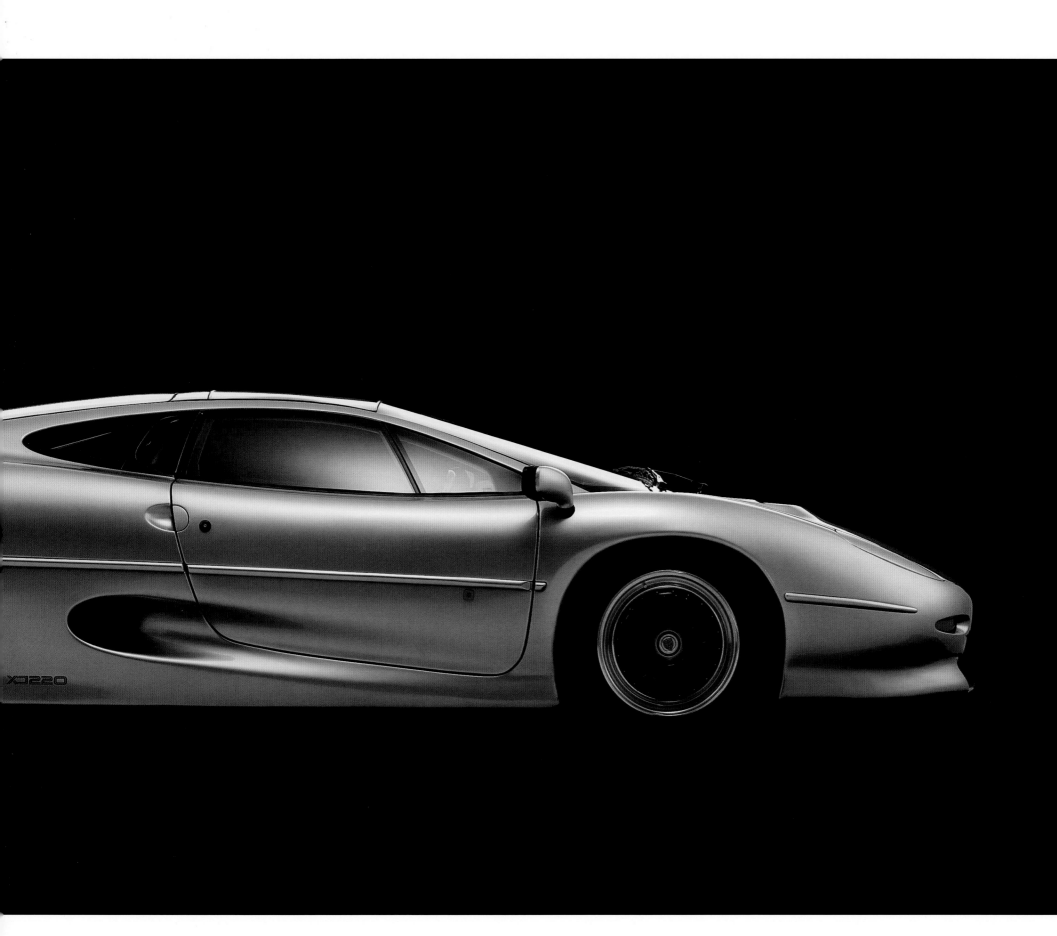

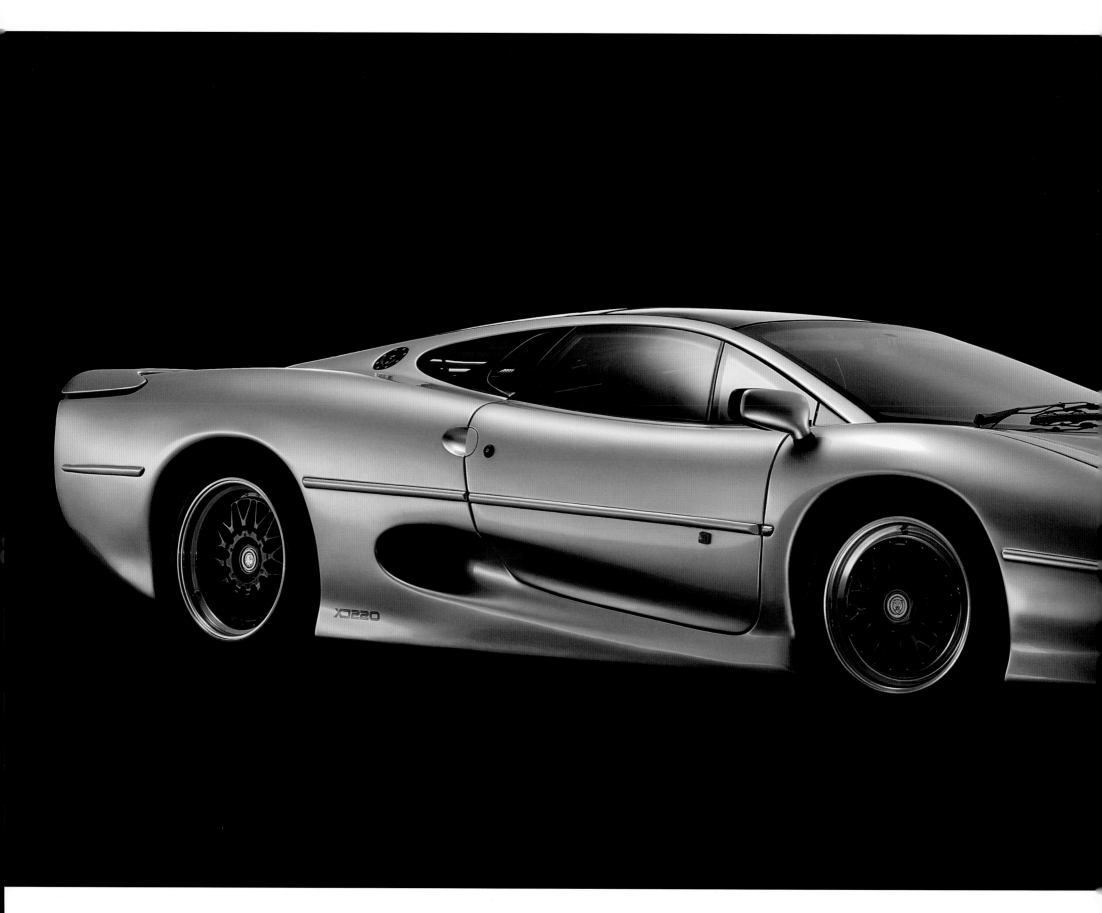

It would be nearly four years before the XJ220 was ready for sale, and in the interim two significant events took place that would have devastating consequences: Firstly, TWR decided to make a fundamental change to the XJ220's specification; and secondly, the bottom dropped out of the global economy. When the XJ220 finally appeared in 1992 its elegantly aerodynamic Geoff Lawson–designed bodyshell sat on a noticeably shorter wheelbase than the concept, making for colossal overhangs front and rear; the scissor doors had been replaced by conventional ones; the 6.2-liter V-12 had become a 3.5-liter twin-turbo V-6; and for many the final straw was that the V-6 transmitted its 542 horsepower through the rear wheels only. Oh, and the price had gone up to £403,000. The imminent McLaren F1 was to be more expensive still, but its performance put the XJ220 well in the shade. The Jaguar was the proverbial hour late and a dollar short.

Of the 1,500-strong putative buyers in the order book, few were to be seen. Tabloid newspapers speculated that angry customers would be demanding their money back. Elton John at least was not among that number, for he kept his XJ220 for nearly nine years, covering just 900 miles and having one very minor but high-profile accident when he hit some traffic cones on the way back from playing tennis.

Had any of those newspaper readers who enjoyed a moment of *schadenfreude* at the musician's expense ever actually sat in the cockpit of an XJ220, they might have viewed his mishap in a more understanding light. Compared with most other supercars of the era it was positively palatial; but, crucially if one was to steer this 5-meter-long, 2-meter-wide beast through an urban environment, the corners are well out of view.

The cabin may be a touch bland by modern standards, but at the time it was almost unheard of to offer comfortable seats in a supercar, or to design the pedal layout to suit anyone other than those few drivers blessed with offset legs. It was quick, too, going from standstill to 62 miles per hour in a claimed 3.6 seconds, and despite its size it weighed just 3,301 pounds (1,375 kg). But it fell short of its 220-mile-per-hour target; Martin Brundle, winner in a Jaguar at Le Mans in 1990, took one up to 217 miles per hour at Nardo, but only after its catalytic converters were removed.

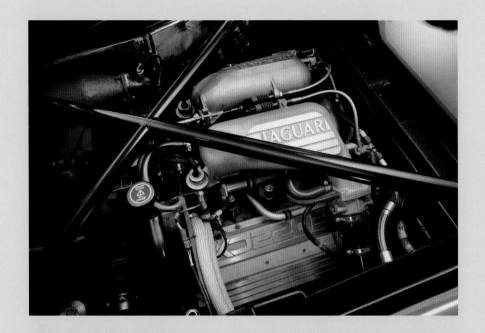

Jaguar Sport had planned a potentially lucrative sideline in the form of the XJ220S, a racer version of the car that could be sold to privateers and used in GT competition. Only five were ever built, and although an XJ220 won its class at Le Mans in 1993 it was already racing under threat of exclusion. The affair is typical of the flexible approach to technical compliance that made Walkinshaw such a controversial figure: In order to run with less aerodynamically draggy 12-inch wheels rather than the 14-inch ones demanded by the Le Mans GT class regs, TWR built the race cars to U.S. IMSA rules. The Le Mans stewards have always taken a poor view of such chicanery, and their riposte to Walkinshaw was to point out that because his race cars had no catalytic converters they were illegal under the IMSA GT rules, which stipulated that if the road car equivalent has catalysts, so must the race car.

Thus Jaguar was permitted to enjoy its class win for two weeks before, no doubt with a *frisson* of delight, the Le Mans organizers ripped up the result.

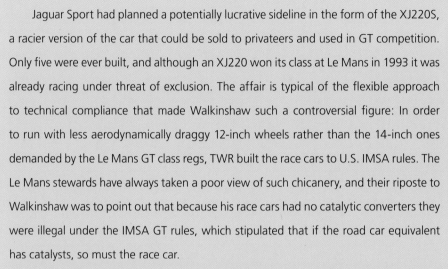

Frank Stephenson

"

They're not actually that expensive today. I'm sure they're going to appreciate in value. It's a classic supercar. There are a couple of things on it that don't do it justice. The mirrors look like they've come off another car. But with a very small redo it would look modern today.

"

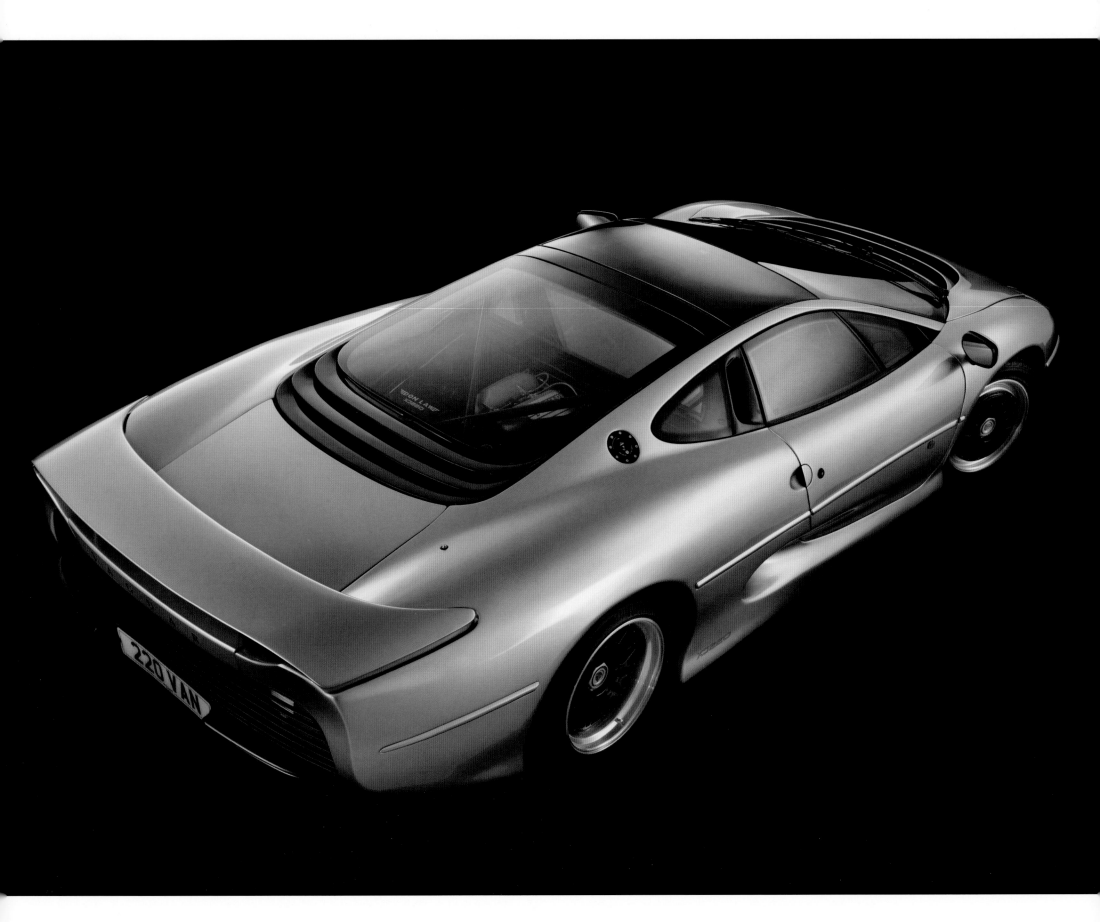

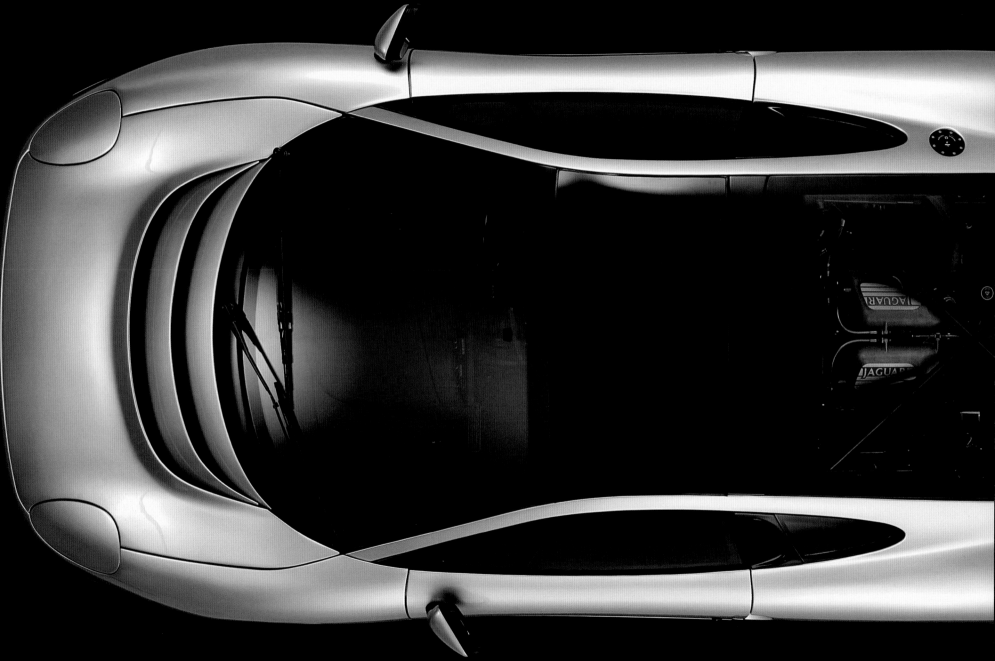

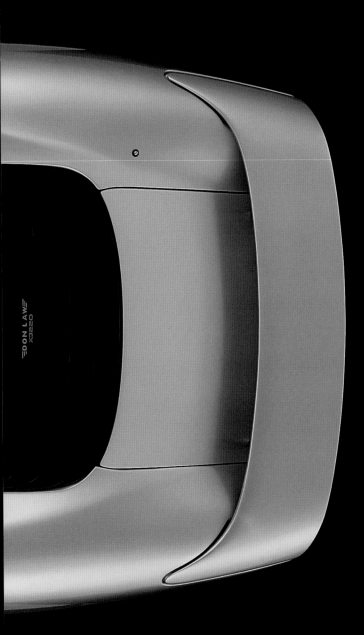

Jaguar XJ220

Years of production	**1992–1993**
Engine	**3.5-liter twin-turbo V-6, 24 valves**
Output	**542 horsepower at 7,200 rpm**
Torque	**473 lb-ft (642 Nm) at 4,500 rpm**
Curb weight	**3,301 pounds (1,375 kg)**
0–60 mph (0–100 kph)	**4 seconds (3.6 seconds)**
Top speed	**217 miles per hour (349 km/hr)**
Number produced	**280**

mclaren
F1

12

Bruce McLaren built his eponymous marque's first road car, the M6GT, with an eye on racing it at the 24 Hours of Le Mans. He was to learn the hard way that the technical framework of sports car racing presents a moving target, since by the time the first prototypes were ready in 1968 a raft of new rules had already rendered the car uncompetitive. In the aftermath of McLaren's untimely death in June 1970, the road car project was shelved. It would remain fallow for two decades.

By 1988, the McLaren team had become one of Formula 1 racing's behemoths under the auspices of Ron Dennis, the former Brabham mechanic who had been installed as McLaren team principal at the behest of their title sponsor in 1980. The MP4/4 won all but one race in the 1988 season, but Gordon Murray, the prodigiously talented engineer who oversaw the project, had declared himself bored and frustrated with the sport's ever more stringent technical regulations. Murray wanted out. Dennis felt he couldn't risk letting his technical director fall into the hands of another team. Something had to give. Dennis therefore sanctioned Murray's pet project: the quickest, best supercar in the world. There would be no half measures; as a patriot as well as a perfectionist, Dennis thoroughly bought in to the concept of designing and building the ultimate supercar in Great Britain.

Murray had at first wanted to design the car himself, but when he came to appreciate the scale of engineering a production car he realized he would need expert collaborators: Steve Rendle, who had worked on the Jaguar XJ220, headed up vehicle dynamics; stylist Peter Stevens and chief engineer Barry Lett were both freelancing after long stints at Lotus; and Harold Dermott, former head of the Midas kit car company, had the necessary composite experience to take charge of production. On March 8, 1990, Murray and his hand-picked team sat around a table for the first time and began the cost-no-object process of designing the F1.

"It's got to look like a McLaren," Murray told Stevens, "although there hasn't been one yet."

> **Frank Stephenson**
>
> This car grew on me. When I first saw it I wasn't taken aback by it, and I don't know why. Now you look at it and see that they really hit the nail on the head, probably because they were going all-out to make it an icon. You can't just go out and build a car like that, using the technology they used, and not expect it to have a huge impact. The amount of aero testing they did was incredible, and the packaging is remarkable.

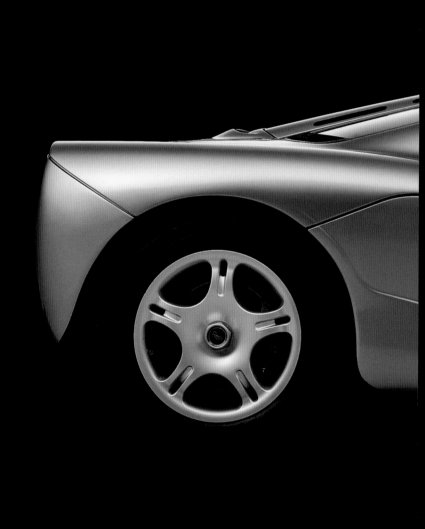

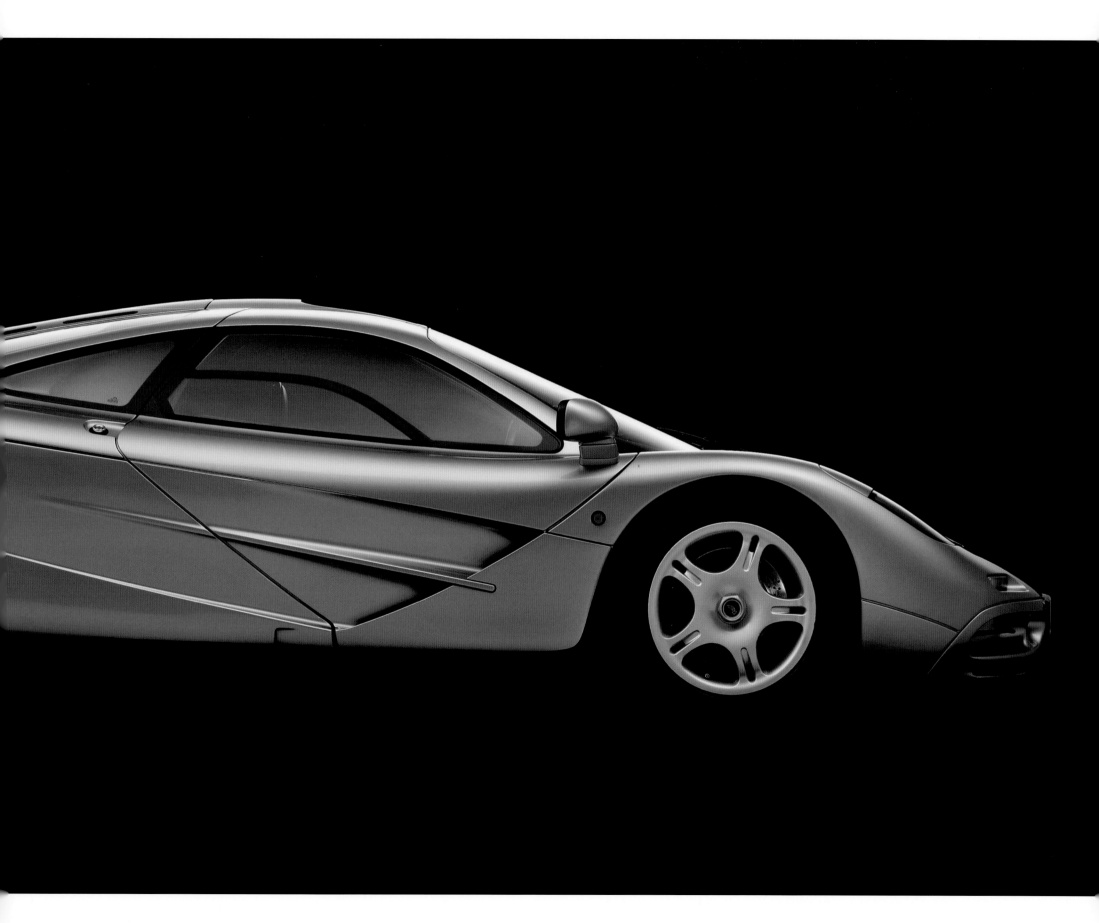

The shape Stevens drew would become iconic. Attention to detail is a McLaren hallmark, and the F1 was exquisitely thought through. The three-seater configuration placed the driver at the center, arriving through a wide door aperture ("The door opening alone would drive most people insane," said Murray of the engineering process), and the main structure was hand-built in carbon fiber. To keep weight down, the seats were shelled in carbon fiber and even the toolkit—not that its putative owners would be the kind of people to risk skinning their knuckles—was titanium. The six-speed gearbox was manual, because above all this was to be a driver's car. BMW provided the mid-mounted engine, a 6.1-liter V-12 that produced 627 horsepower at 7,400 rpm, although engine guru Paul Rosche offered to fit a turbocharger as well. Since the F1's curb weight was a mere 2,502 pounds (1,140 kg), giving a power-to-weight ratio of 550 horsepower per metric ton, Murray wisely demurred.

The F1 used ground effect aerodynamics—long since banned in Formula 1—to

Frank Stephenson

"

I hadn't actually sat in one until recently, when the owners club came here [to the McLaren Technology Centre] to celebrate the 20th anniversary of the start of development. I used to be a non-believer in the central driving position. I couldn't see what the fuss was all about. Have you ever sat in a McLaren F1? Do it! I sat in one and my whole perception changed, right there. You sit in it and you think, 'I could go really fast in this car, *comfortably*.'

"

provide downforce and stability, and the production car was electronically limited to a top speed of 230 miles per hour. In March 1998, one of the original prototypes clocked 240.1 miles per hour on a private test track in the hands of sports car racer Andy Wallace; the F1 was indisputably the fastest production car in the world, a position it would enjoy until the Bugatti Veyron unseated it.

During the F1's gestation, though, the world tilted sharply on its economic axis, and by the time the car was ready for launch in 1993 there was less of an appetite than before for supercars, let alone one whose carbon fiber monocoque took 3,000 hours to construct, leading to an eye-watering price of £540,000. The F1 drew plaudits for its performance and driver-focused fluency ("That a two-wheel-drive car can generate the grip, produce the chassis composure and still have enough talent left to post a 0–60 mph time of just 3.2 seconds is a feat that may stand for all time," wrote *Autocar*, the only magazine given carte blanche to conduct a measured performance test) but found

> ### Frank Stephenson
>
> It was designed to be *tight*, and I think that's a common factor in the really great supercars. They're more believable if they're less *styled*. Like military aircraft—nobody comes in and tries to make them look beautiful, they just try to make them perform in the best possible way. There isn't any piece of superfluous design on the F1: form equals function.

Frank Stephenson

"

There are a few little things on it that they didn't make themselves, like the indicators. They don't really change the car at all. I think it looks timeless—it's always going to look good, no matter what. It's very characterful. And the beauty of it is that it's so compact. Okay, the front overhang isn't as short as you'd think, but they had to fit the radiators in.

"

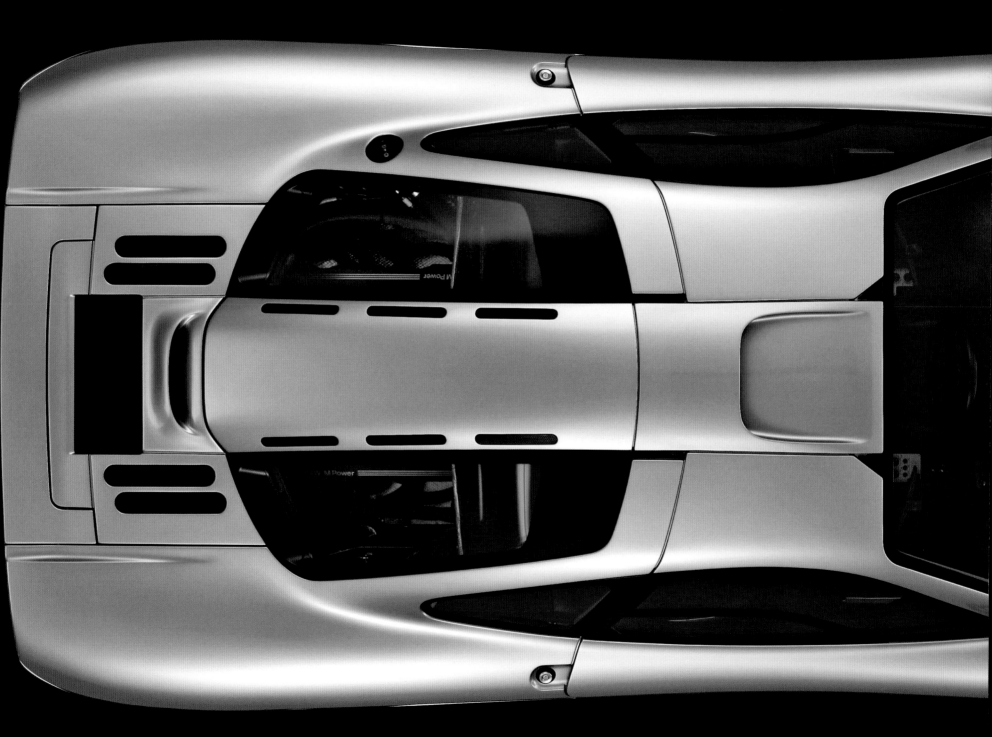

its way into far fewer garages than McLaren had originally envisaged.

The F1 had not been designed with racing in mind, but sluggish sales prompted McLaren to entertain requests from wealthy privateers for a racing variant. A more potent engine and modified body panels, including a longer tail, distinguished the F1 GTR that arrived in 1995. The car would feature strongly on the international GT racing scene for several seasons, but its finest hour came at rain-lashed Le Mans in 1995, when a team of drivers led by ex-F1 star J. J. Lehto won the race convincingly.

Production ended in 1998, and in the final reckoning 65 F1s were sold (64 during the production run, with the Park Lane showroom car following in 2004), plus 28 GTRs and a further five of the special-edition LMs that were built to celebrate that Le Mans victory. Over the following decade, as the economic chill faded into memory, the F1's relative scarcity made it an attractive investment for the super-rich. On the rare occasions they come to market, F1s now fetch seven-figure sums.

McLaren F1	
Years of production	**1993–1998**
Engine	**6.1-liter BMW V-12**
Output	**627 horsepower at 7,400 rpm**
Torque	**455 lb-ft (617 Nm) at 4,000 rpm**
Curb weight	**2,502 pounds (1,140 kg)**
0–60 mph	**3.2 seconds**
Top speed	**230 miles per hour (370 kph)**
Number produced	**65**

ferrari
F50

13

For reasons that are hard to quantify, the F50 has become Ferrari's forgotten supercar. Following the success of the F40, which had been built to celebrate Ferrari's 40th anniversary as a car manufacturer and proved so popular that production lasted until 1992, some sort of follow-up was inevitable. And yet when Ferrari unveiled the F50 at the 1995 Geneva show—two years before the 50th anniversary—it put a firm cap on production. Market research indicated demand of 350 units, it said, so 349 would be made. F40 production had expanded from the projected 400 units to 1,315. . . .

The F50 was a logical extension of the F40 concept as an F1 car for the road, including a V-12 engine that was actually derived from a contemporary Formula 1 car. This not only made the F50 longer and slightly wider than the twin-turbo V-8 F40, it made it considerably more expensive—$500,000—at a time when the world was in recession. The kind of person who can afford to spend $500,000 on such a car may not be reduced to outright penury during times of global economic hardship, but they often have compelling reasons not to flaunt their wealth—at least until conspicuous consumption becomes fashionable again.

Pininfarina composed a shape that was a more curvaceous evolution of the F40's chiseled wedge, with the signature tail spoiler adorning a rear deck that was longer to accommodate the V-12 and its transmission (although competitive expediency would prompt Scuderia Ferrari to switch to V-10 engines in F1 from the 1996 season onward). It was the F50's sheer width (78.2 inches) that many found intimidating; this was not a car that could be threaded delicately along narrow, twisting roads.

Frank Stephenson

This car never did it for me. I know it's a fantastic car to drive, better than the F40, and one of the best sports cars of its time—but to look at it, it's a bit . . . soapy, you know, like you stuck it in the oven and it melted. There isn't enough tension in the body, although I like the wraparound glass.

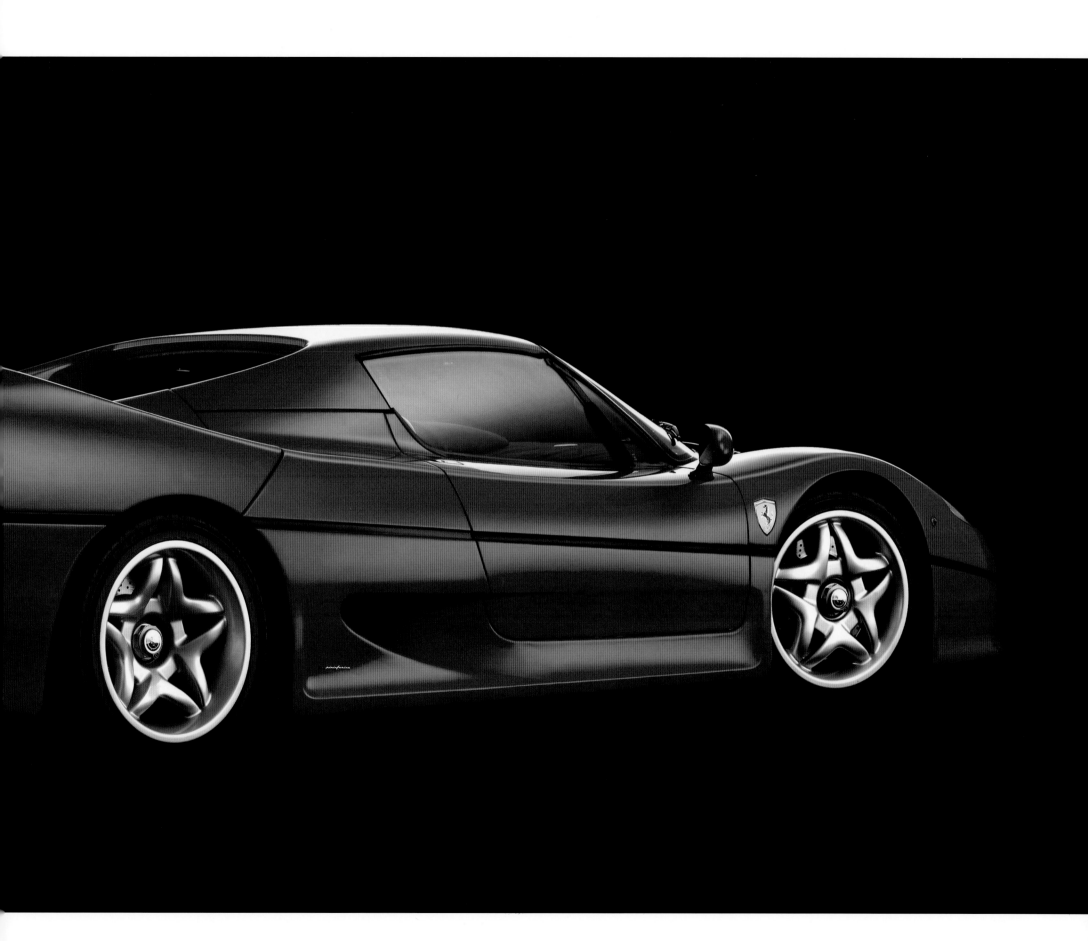

There were more creature comforts than the F40: wind-up windows and a neatly trimmed, if Spartan, dashboard. The interior carbon fiber panels were lacquered and glossy rather than unfinished, and the carbon fiber seat had a modicum of padding. Elsewhere, though, the F50 stuck close to the racing ethic. The chassis was once again a space frame clothed in lightweight composite panels, with the engine acting as a stressed member and bolted directly to the bulkhead, as it would in an F1 car, while it and the transmission also carried the rear suspension pickups. At 2,712 pounds (1,230 kg) it belied its physical size, although the mass of the engine brought the distribution to 42:58.

The 60-valve quad-cam V-12 was based on the architecture of the 1994 F1 engine but enlarged from 3.5 liters to 4.7 and mated to a six-speed manual gearbox rather than a semi-automatic. Those looking forward to an F1-style redline in the late teens would be disappointed: The production V-12 hit the limiter at 8,500 rpm, only 500

Frank Stephenson

" It was a dramatic departure from the language of the Enzo, but I think they went too far. It's not sensual enough. If the F40 looks like a car that went to the gym, the F50 is kind of like the F40 after it quit going to the gym and started going soft. It looks overweight rather than muscular. "

revs after developing its peak power of 513 horsepower. The F50 achieved the metric zero to 100 km/h (zero to 62 miles per hour) in 3.7 seconds and, given an adequately long and unpopulated road, could reach 202 miles per hour, so on paper it was only an incremental advance on its older brother.

Comparisons between the F40 and F50 became irrelevant once the V-12 fired into life, for this is where the F50 firmly established the uniqueness of its character. A Ferrari V-12 sounds like no other on earth, especially when mounted immediately behind the driver's head and responding as if the two were wired together. This was a far more competent, connected, and communicative supercar than its savagely dramatic predecessor.

Ferrari also developed a variant of the car for sports car racing, a popular category for gentlemen racers with the wherewithal to purchase the marque's products. The F50 GT weighed in at under 1,000kg and its engine was brought closer to racing spec to

Frank Stephenson

"
For me, take the body off and there's an amazing car underneath. Engine, technology—everything was good on that car, and it set the bar higher when it came out.
"

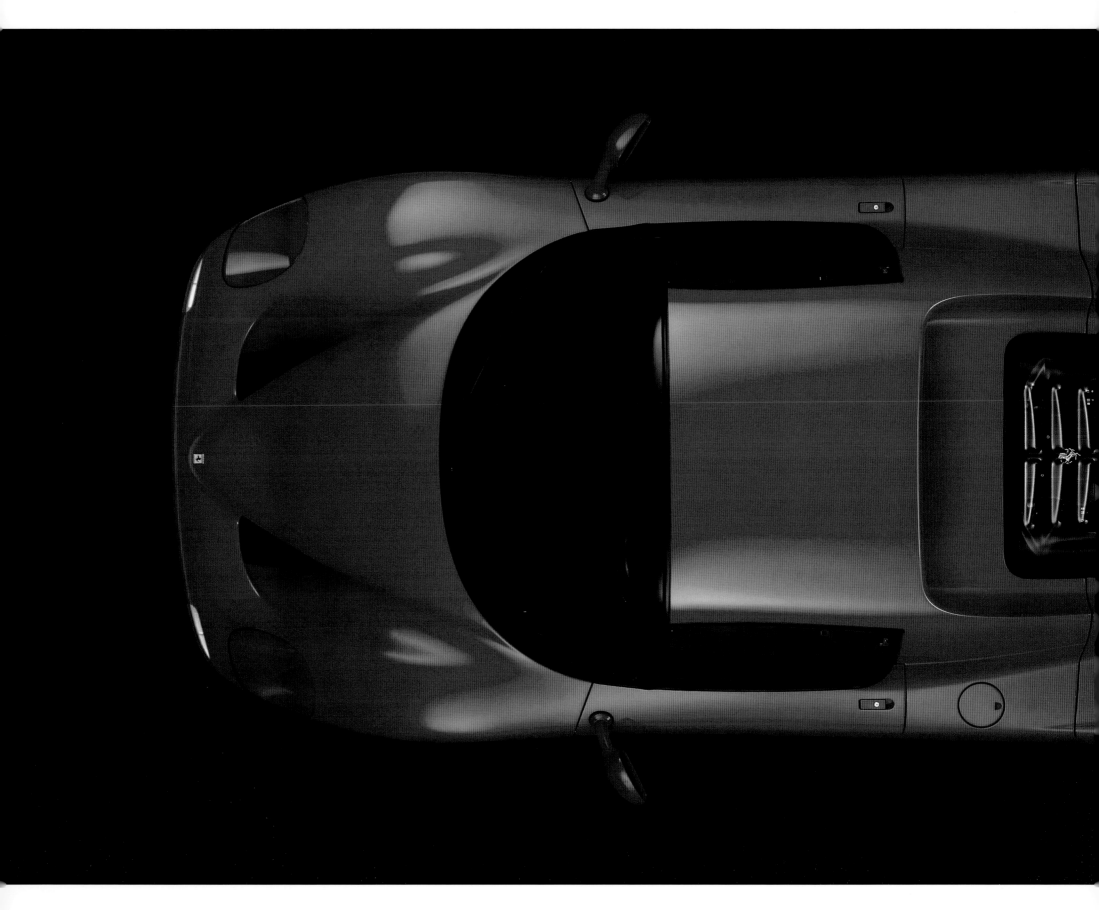

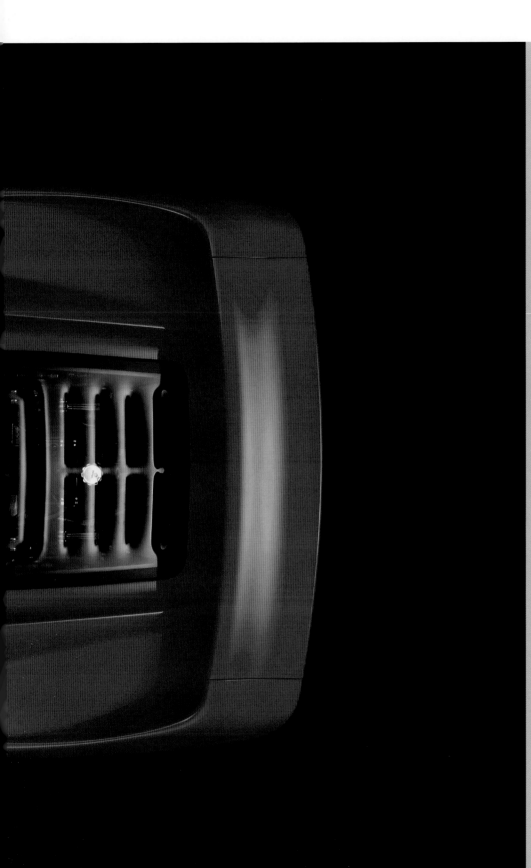

produce 750 horsepower, but its completion coincided with a change in management at Maranello. Jean Todt was brought in to turn Ferrari's racing fortunes around—in the years between the launches of the F40 and F50 it had won but 13 Grands Prix—and the company's focus inevitably shifted toward F1. The 333SP sports prototype project was left to Dallara and Michelotto and the in-house F50 project withered on the vine. Production of the F50 ended as planned, with the 349th car. Every one of them had been sold—and, of course, loved.

Ferrari F50

Years of production	**1995–1997**
Engine	**4-7-liter DOHC 65-degree V-12**
Output	**513 horsepower at 8,000 rpm**
Torque	**347 lb-ft (470 Nm) at 6,500 rpm**
Curb weight	**2,712 pounds (1,230 kg)**
0–62 mph/0–100 kph	**3.7 seconds**
Top speed	**202 miles per hour (325 kph)**
Number produced	**349**

porsche
CARRERA GT

14

Sports cars don't necessarily have to be clever. For many customers, speed is the most prized quality; and for many manufacturers, tradition often wins over innovation. And of all the leading sports car makers it is Porsche, perhaps, that best demonstrates this eternal conflict. Here is a company so determined to preserve the essential Ludditism of locating the engine of its most long-lived model, the 911, in the wrong place (slightly aft of the rear wheels) that it has had to invest decades and untold engineering resources fighting the laws of physics. The result is that you can now, while pressing on, back off the 911's throttle mid-bend without its tail making an abrupt lunge for the scenery.

In motorsport, Porsche's determination to plow its own furrow has meant more than one failure in Formula 1; its last venture at the top level, an overweight V-12 where the power takeoff was from the center of the crankshaft rather than the end (which solved the problem of the crankshaft twisting but enforced a high center of gravity, which is why nobody else had done it in the sport since the 1950s) ended in outright humiliation. And yet its expertise in turbocharging and cautious advancement of its flat-six engine format has yielded countless victories in the 24 Hours of Le Mans.

So while the 959 of the 1980s noticeably upped the technological ante (principally to get over the hurdle of keeping the engine behind the rear wheels), no other Porsche supercar epitomizes the Stuttgart marque's on/off relationship with motorsport like the Carrera GT. It was born from the ashes of a Le Mans car that never raced; it was ridiculously quick and efficient, cutting-edge in many ways, had its engine in the right place, and yet is almost Porsche's forgotten supercar.

Porsche had taken class victories at Le Mans, and other grueling endurance events such as the Carrera Panamericana, before launching an all-out assault on the overall Le Mans win in the late 1960s. Its 917 racer, engineered by Ferry Porsche's grandson Ferdinand Piëch (latterly head of the VW group), was dangerously unstable in its first incarnation but delivered the goods in 1970 and 1971. It gave the rule-makers such a fright that the regulations were adjusted to keep it out. Porsche's 956 and 962 redefined sports car racing in the 1980s; they were the quintessential turn-key racers, competitive in the hands of privateer teams and filling out the Le Mans grid in the lean years as well as dominating the race for overall honors. Porsche won again in the 1990s, first with the WSC 95, a curious TWR-built "bitsa," which was actually based around the tub of the Jaguar XJR-14, and then with the 911 GT1 in 1998.

The 911 GT1's win was something of a fluke that owed more to the endurance racing *nous* of its drivers and unreliability of its rivals than to the car's outright pace. The balance of the regulations now favored open-top cars rather than closed-cockpit ones.

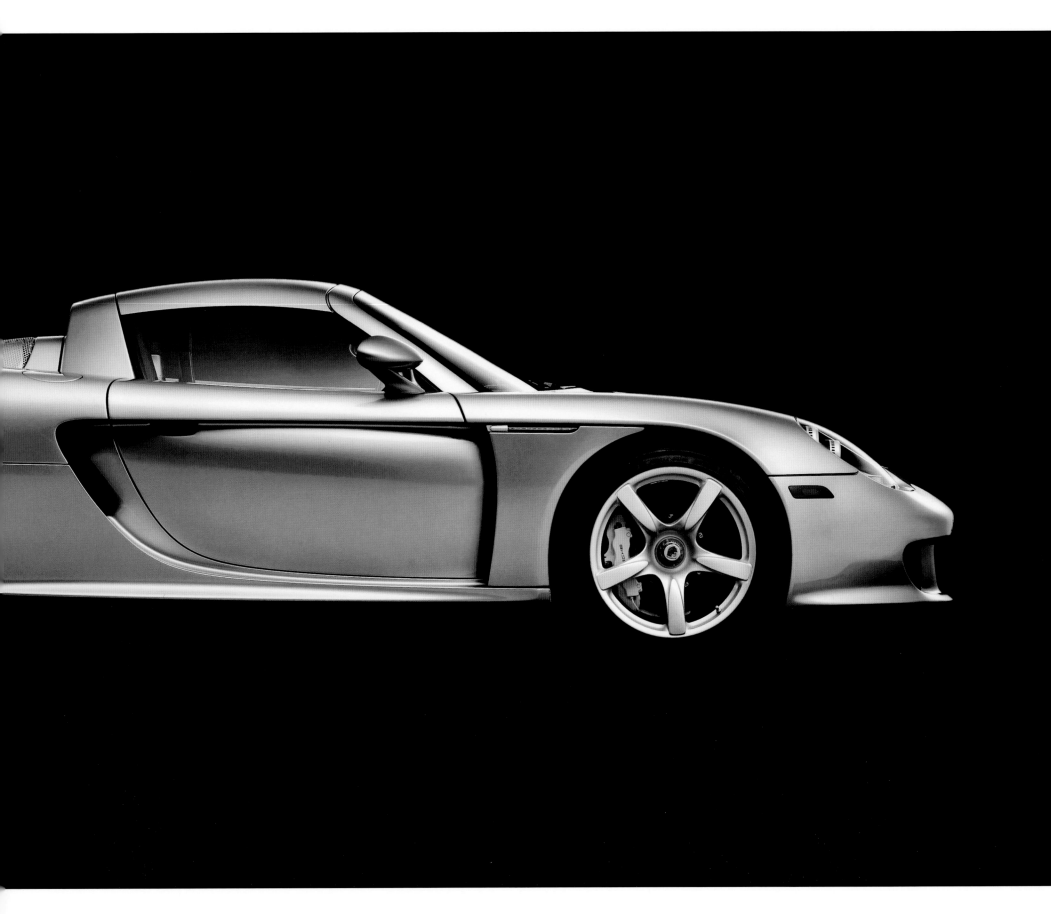

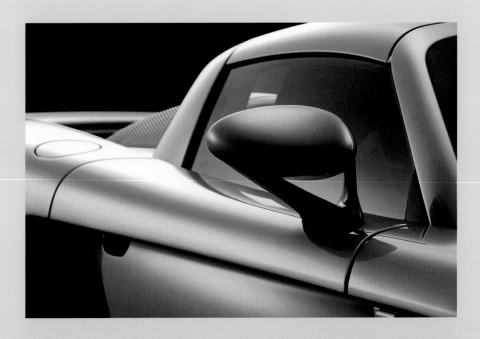

There was some excitement, therefore, when in early 2000 grainy spy shots circulated of what could only be a Porsche open-top prototype, the tartan sweep across the driver's crash helmet indicating that 1998 Le Mans winner Allan McNish was at the wheel.

That car, though, would never be seen again. The project was canned since it was deemed a waste of resources to compete with Audi, which was then embarking on a long-term Le Mans campaign, and yet another rule change meant that high-capacity engines such as the putative racer's 5.5-liter V-10 would be restricted more than small-capacity turbo engines. The money went to fund the Cayenne SUV instead.

But, having built a carbon tub and a V-10 engine to sit amidships, Porsche could hardly consign them to the scrapper. Purists may loathe the Cayennes and all who sail in them, but over the intervening years they have come to appreciate the enabling effects of that model's strong sales. The Carrera GT might never have come about without it.

To meet emissions regulations the V-10 required an additional piston ring and a longer stroke, so Porsche brought it out to 5.7 liters. In most other respects it was left as it would be in the race car, which is what gives the Carrera GT its almost savage character. It makes the zero-to-62-mile-per-hour benchmark sprint in a neck-snapping 3.9 seconds; and with minimal flywheel effect it can be made to decelerate almost as sharply simply by lifting off the throttle. The clutch is carbon-ceramic and so light that Porsche recommended owners not apply the throttle until it was fully engaged when moving off from a standstill, the better to avoid an unplanned interface with any obstacles nearby.

When the Carrera GT was released to the public at the tail end of 2003, it provoked a stampede of speculators. To deter profiteers, who would look to sell early cars on at a markup to enthusiasts further down the queue, Porsche prioritized existing customers and demanded a £25,000 down payment even before contracts were signed, followed by another £25k when specifying the car.

Frank Stephenson

" This was their supercar to compete with the Enzo. It's instantly recognizable as a Porsche, and done very well—more intelligent than the 959, I think, in terms of design. For me, it's important that a car looks like it comes from the company that made it. This car looks great and it has the Porsche DNA. The interior is nice too, although they took a lot of weight out of the car so it's quite basic. You get a nice wooden shift lever, though. "

Unfortunately this 612-horsepower beast would not have the roads to itself for long. Ferrari's Enzo played strongly on its F1 links; that, plus its undoubted visual drama, enabled it to steal the light from the better-finished but more conservatively styled Porsche.

Still, as Jeremy Clarkson wrote of the Carrera GT in his road test for the *Sunday Times*, "This, quite simply, is as good as it gets." The Carrera GT may make fewer nods to Porsche's heritage than you would expect—the birchwood top of the gear lever acknowledges the 917—but it was certainly clever. And, of course, supremely fast.

Frank Stephenson

"

It had a very short lifespan—it's as if everyone's forgotten about it. It was good when it came out and then other cars arrived which were at an even higher level than that.

"

151

Porsche Carrera GT

Years of production	**2003–2006**
Engine	**5.7-liter DOHC 68-degree V-10, 40 valves**
Output	**612 horsepower at 8,000 rpm**
Torque	**435 lb-ft (590 Nm) at 5,750 rpm**
Curb weight	**3,042 pounds (1,380 kg)**
0–62 mph/0–100 kph	**3.9 seconds**
Top speed	**205 miles per hour (330 kph)**
Number produced	**1,270**

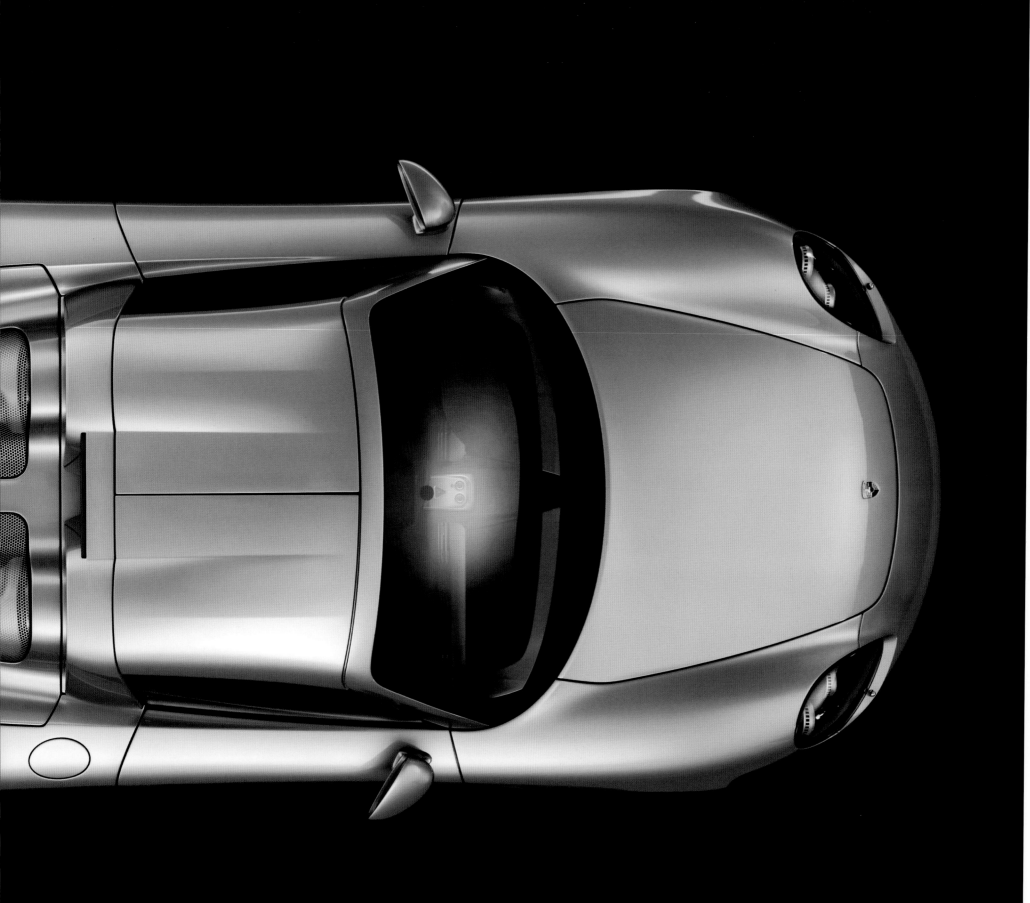

maserati
MC12

n the 1950s, Maserati fought Ferrari and Mercedes for domination of the world's racetracks, but it overextended itself and paid the price. Almost all the clichés of Italian business are enshrined within its history: a family enterprise, crafting exquisitely styled products with passion (if not the very best of actual raw materials); a palace coup staged by a shady businessman; bankruptcy, uncertain ownership, and industrial unrest; failed attempts to break into a broader market; and finally a comfortable return to basics under the shelter of a greater corporate wing.

Alfieri, Bindo, Ernesto, and Ettore Maserati built quick racing cars during the 1920s and 1930s, but their finances were always shaky. Alfieri died in 1932, and the fascist-aligned industrialist Alberto Orsi bought the remaining brothers out in 1937, retaining them as employees on 10-year contracts. In very short order, Orsi relocated the company from Bologna to Modena and recruited new engineers from elsewhere.

Despite further successes on track—Wilbur Shaw took two of his three Indianapolis 500 victories at the wheel of Maseratis—the brothers took their leave when their contracts ran out in 1947.

The 1950s were characterized by rapid expansion, increasingly strained industrial relations, and, ultimately, financial ruin. The 250F became a favorite among Formula 1 drivers, albeit more for its sweet handling than its quality of construction or reliability. Orsi's arbitrary treatment of his employees—locking them out of the factory, for instance, to weed out those with suspected Communist sympathies—provoked strikes and harmed productivity, but it was an ill-judged foreign enterprise that brought Maserati to the brink. Orsi leveraged the business to facilitate a lucrative tooling contract with the Perón regime in Argentina; after Perón was deposed in 1955 and the incoming government defaulted on repayments, the creditors moved in.

Somehow Orsi clung on to the reins and the company refocused on road cars. The Ghibli of 1967, styled by a young Giorgetto Giugiaro, was a sales hit, but Maserati was about to enter another period of turbulence. Citroën took a 60-percent stake in the company at the end of 1967 and bought Orsi out entirely in 1971. This marriage begat the eccentric Maserati-engined Citroën SM as well as the Bora, a mid-engined two-seater that would be Maserati's first mass-produced sports car.

Sadly, the Bora and its siblings, the Merak (a 2+2 version of the Bora with a smaller engine) and the Khamsin (a front-engined GT), were never built in the quantities envisaged. Although more workers were hired, a succession of strikes meant that productivity slumped. The SM was such a niche car that it was never likely to sell in sufficient quantities to recoup its development costs, and then the 1973 oil crisis tipped Citroën over the edge. The French government engineered a merger with Peugeot, whose bean counters embarked upon an almost Stalinist purge of Citroën's history and inventory. Spare Maserati V-6 blocks for the SM were destroyed by being pushed out of a warehouse window.

Argentine industrialist Alejandro De Tomaso acquired the remnants of Maserati with financial assistance from the Italian government. New models arrived but the 1970s were not a happy decade, particularly for veteran engineer Giulio Alfieri, who reputedly learned that his services were no longer required when he arrived for work and found the contents of his desk sitting outside.

By the time Fiat bought the company from De Tomaso in 1993, Maserati's reputation was as tatty as its aging model lineup. What the marque needed was credibility. The 3200GT of 1998 combined crisp Giugiaro styling with a characterful 3.2-liter twin-turbo V-8 whose enthusiastic power delivery regularly overwhelmed the more modest capabilities of the chassis. Still, Maserati had found its niche as a kind of junior Ferrari, and under Maranello's stewardship its fortunes continued to improve.

The Ferrari connection brought investment and engineering rigor, but above all it enabled Maserati to target markets it had not dared consider for decades. Until the

> ### Frank Stephenson
>
> I enjoyed working on this car a lot. I've got to say I don't agree with the graphic scheme on this particular example. I did a similar one, and the reason for the blue at the back is that it's such a long car, the blue takes about a foot off the overall length when you look at the side view. What I don't really like is that sharp 'tooth' on the door [at the leading edge of the window]. It's there for structural reasons, but we disguised it with a graphic that came down and made it look much cleaner, like the glass just wrapped around.

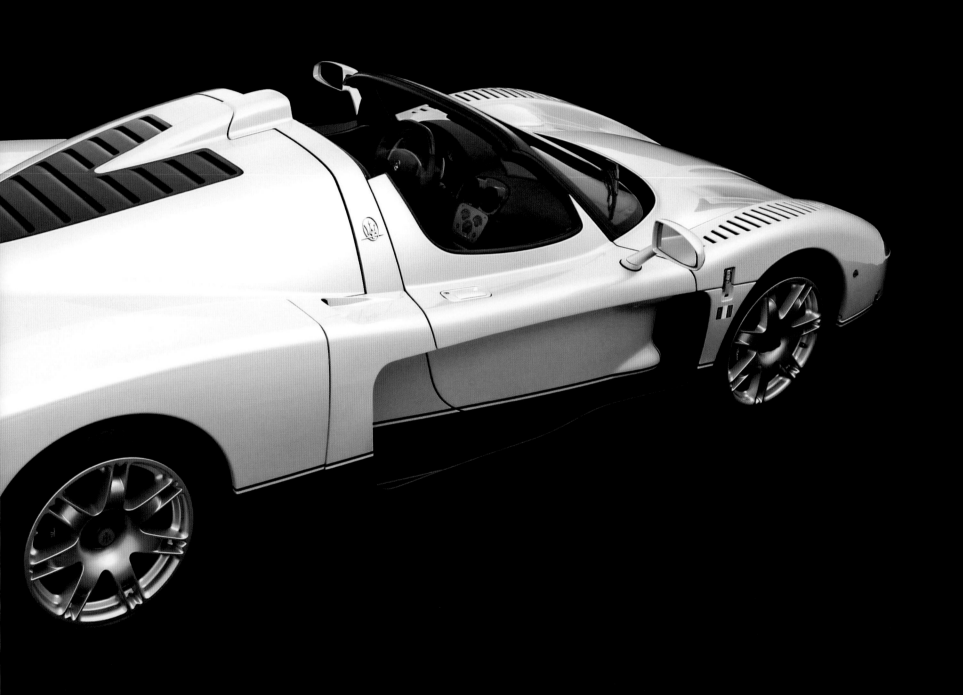

1950s, it had sought to turn a profit by building customer racing cars; now it could do so again as a sideline to its burgeoning road car range. Based on the same carbon fiber "tub" as the Ferrari Enzo and sharing many of the mechanicals, the MC12 really was a race car for the road—a homologation special of which a minimum 25 had to be built in order for the race version to qualify for international GT racing. Ultimately 50 were built between 2004 and 2005.

The shared componentry with the Enzo led to many fatuous comparisons between the two cars. Standing 17.4 inches (44 cm) longer than the Enzo—of which 5.9 inches (15 cm) were in the wheelbase—2.4 (6 cm) wider and 2.2 (6 cm) taller, the MC 12 was never going to match the Ferrari's agility around a tight course. The shape, honed by Frank Stephenson from Giugiaro's initial concept, swept back to a longer tail for less drag at high speeds.

Inside, the MC12 was not so much more luxuriously finished as . . . finished—in that the Enzo's cockpit was stark, functional, and heavy on the carbon fiber. The MC12 at least made an effort to cosset with some soft-feel furnishings, although the presence of the rollover bar was a permanent reminder of the racing heritage.

Although it bore more of the trappings of a grand tourer than the Enzo, the MC12's minimal luggage accommodation would still require its (wealthy) owners to send their cases on ahead if they were planning more than an overnight stay. No, to properly assess the nuances that genuinely separated the Maserati from the Ferrari would require more than a detailed look at the technical specifications.

Perhaps the most revealing comparison between the MC12 and the Enzo came on the BBC program *Top Gear*, in which The Stig, the show's resident racing driver, drove both cars around the same course. The MC12 was a tenth of a second faster than the Ferrari that had sired it; a small margin, but one that the Maserati brothers would no doubt have approved of.

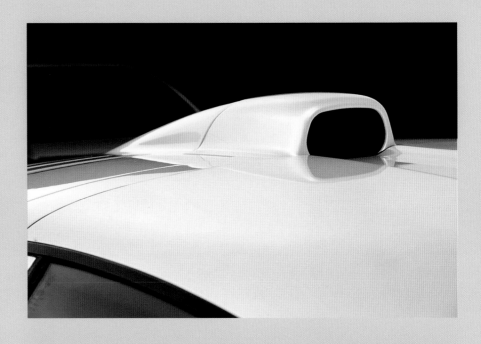

Frank Stephenson

"

It had the [Ferrari] Enzo basis but we extended the wheelbase in front, so overall it was quite a bit longer than the Enzo. I loved working on this project because when I came in, it was just a concept on a piece of paper, and Giorgio Ascanelli [ex-McLaren and Ferrari Formula 1 race engineer] said, 'Well, would you like to do it?' And of course I said yes. Obviously we had to build 25 road cars for homologation, but while the other GT1 manufacturers were making their road cars into race cars, we went the back way: We made the race car into a road car.

"

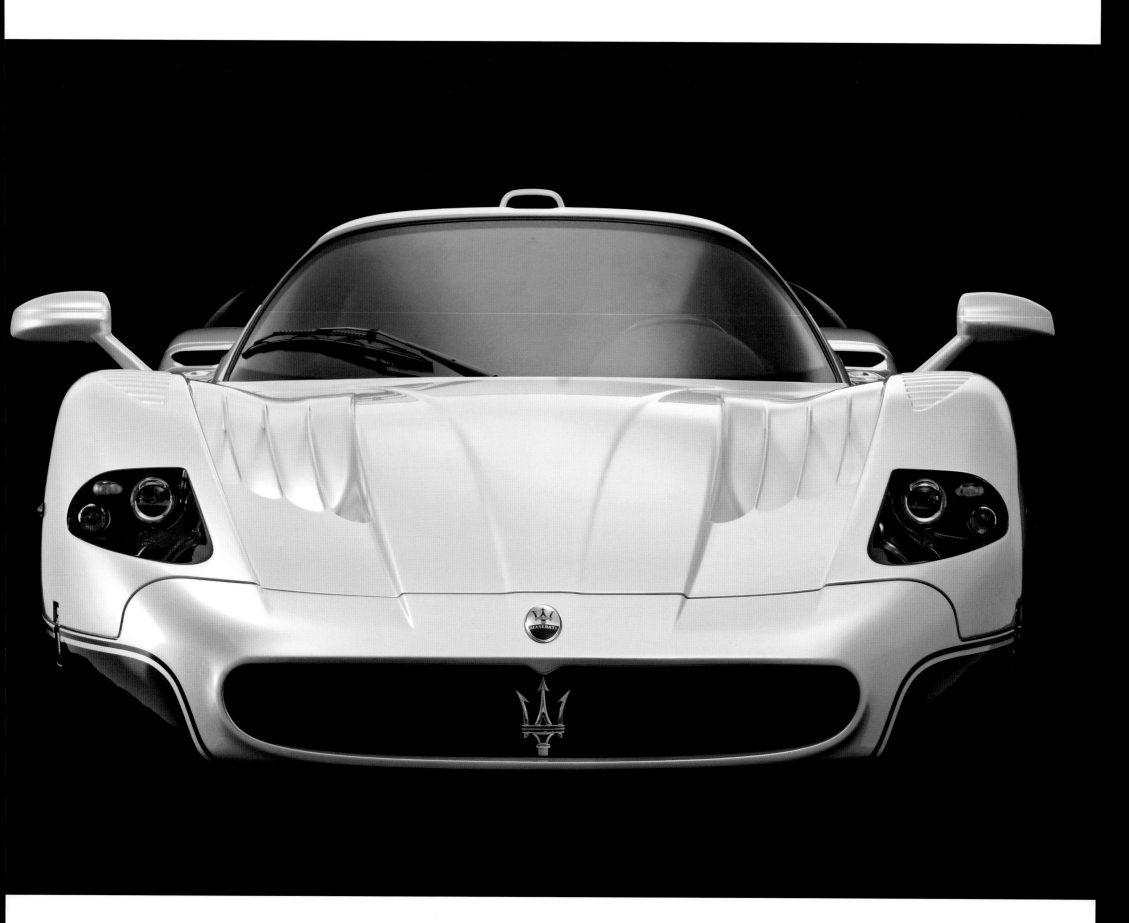

Frank Stephenson

"

Some people say it was a rip-off of the Ferrari—it wasn't. There was so much that was different, and that was our challenge—to make it different, to make it look like a Maserati. I was a huge fan of Group C sports car racing, and the brief was that so long as the aerodynamics worked, we could do what we wanted. The snorkel and the long tail are very Le Mans—the only frustration was having to use taillights and headlights out of a catalog rather than designing our own. But it had a real Italian warmth to it.

"

Maserati MC12

Years of production	**2004–2005**
Engine	**6.0-liter DOHC 90-degree V-12**
Output	**632 horsepower at 7,500 rpm**
Torque	**481 lb-ft (652 Nm)**
Curb weight	**2,945 pounds (1,336 kg)**
0–60 mph	**3.7 seconds**
Top speed	**205 miles per hour (330 kph)**
Number produced	**50**

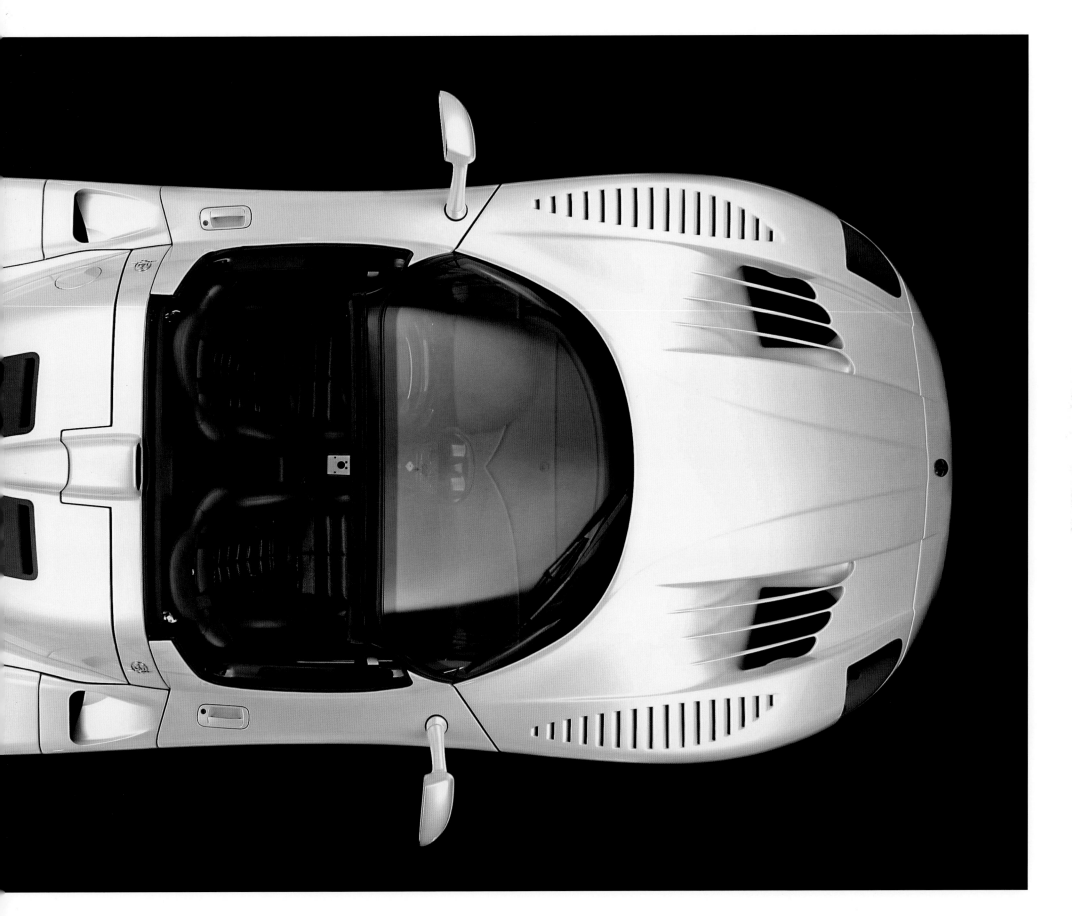

bugatti
VEYRON
16.4

Although many historic names have vanished and then been reborn bearing only a badge in common with past glories, one could never accuse this marque—now part of the Volkswagen Group—of deviating from Ettore Bugatti's rarefied philosophy. And while Bugatti and his successors were long gone by the time the Veyron was conceived, this gloriously irrelevant 1,001-horsepower beast owes its existence to a scion of another famous motoring dynasty.

Between 1909 and 1947, Ettore Bugatti produced lovingly crafted sports and racing cars in tiny volumes in his workshops at Molsheim in Alsace, France. They were characterized by exquisite attention to detail and—for the time—extraordinary performance. The Type 35 was arguably his greatest creation; he built around 400 of this and derivative specifications between 1924 and 1931, and they dominated the pre-war Grand Prix racing

Frank Stephenson

" I like the shape of this car. The guy who modeled it was actually the same guy who modeled the [new] MINI. I can see a lot of his touches in it. He has a good feel for surfaces—there's just enough puffiness in it without going too heavy. "

scene. Bugattis also won the 24 Hours of Le Mans in 1937 and 1939, the latter victory arriving thanks to the efforts of drivers Jean-Pierre Wimille and Pierre Veyron.

World War II wrought devastation on the Alsace region and Bugatti's factory was destroyed. Ettore died in 1947, and while his son Roland attempted to keep the marque alive—there was even an attempted Grand Prix comeback in 1956—the company had to abandon car manufacture in favor of making aircraft components. The name sank into the murk of history until Italian entrepreneur Romano Artioli bought it in 1987.

The rapid infusion of cash under Artioli yielded a bespoke new factory near Modena in Italy, and the new car, the EB110, was heavy on carbon fiber but light on styling finesse, even though the pen of Marcello Gandini was allegedly involved. Artioli also established a luxury-goods brand trading under the Bugatti name, but his ill-advised acquisition of Lotus in 1993 proved an expansion too far. By the time the EB110 was launched, the world was well into recession and Artioli's empire went spectacularly bust in 1995.

Three years later, the Volkswagen Group, under the leadership of Ferdinand Piëch, bought the rights to the Bugatti name and embarked on an ambitious series of concept cars, testing the market for what could prove to be the ultimate supercar. In 2000, Piëch officially announced the Veyron at the Geneva motor show with a clear statement of intent that it would be the fastest, most powerful, and most exclusive supercar ever—more so even than the McLaren F1. For Piëch, the engineer behind the Porsche 917, this would be a last hurrah after several decades establishing VW as a global player. But like the VW Phaeton, a mothership-sized luxury sedan that never sold in the numbers projected, the new Bugatti would prove to be a costly and troublesome vanity project.

· The Veyron—named after the 1939 Le Mans winner—ran way over budget and was plagued by development problems as the VW Group's finest engineers attempted to cure its wanton lack of high-speed stability. With a mid-mounted W-16 engine (essentially two V-8s conjoined at the crank) imbibing charged air from four turbos and

Frank Stephenson

" It looks to me like a bully, like the kid in class who's two inches taller than everybody else and 20 pounds heavier. Then again, he dresses nice even though he comes from the wrong side of the tracks! "

a curb weight of 4,162 pounds (1,888 kg), the Veyron posed questions for which the laws of physics could only offer a dramatic retort.

When former BMW executive Bernd Pischetsrieder succeeded Piëch as VW chairman in 2002, the Veyron project was still deep in the mire. But Pischetsrieder, very much a car man rather than a bean counter, elected to push on to completion rather than cancel it. He installed former banker and gentleman racer Thomas Bscher at the helm of Bugatti and brought in fresh engineering eyes to solve its stability issues.

The Veyron was ready to meet its public in 2006. Where the McLaren F1 used the velvet glove of Formula 1–derived ground effect aerodynamics to balance a drag coefficient of 0.32 with stability-inducing downforce, the heavier and less aero-efficient Veyron relied on the clunking fist of its ludicrous quad-turbo W-16 to bludgeon its way to a quoted top speed of 252 miles per hour.

A price tag in the region of $1.7 million ensured that potential owners were among

> ### *Frank Stephenson*
>
> "
>
> It's an incredible car and you can play with the graphics all day—you can see the color coding on this one. Breaking up the color components makes it feel smaller. And there's a lot of designed technology on it—the intakes, the little arms that raise the spoiler are designed to be beautiful. Whether it's light or not I don't know, but when you're putting down 1,000 horsepower you probably put that on the back burner. . .
>
> "

the super-rich rather than the merely wealthy. Even so, the Veyron was never likely to recoup the staggering costs incurred during its protracted development. It was almost inevitable that once the project's cheerleaders had moved on, new management would usher it toward the off-ramp.

"One rule we have to follow in the future is that every product has to make money," said Pischetsrieder's successor, Wendelin Wiedeking, in 2007.

This was not quite the epitaph for the fastest road car of all time. Bugatti announced a limited-run Super Sport model, literally the Veyron to end all Veyrons, with more power (1,183 horses) from a substantially reworked engine and a chassis that had been reworked from the ground up.

In July 2010, Bugatti test driver Pierre-Henri Raphanel girded his loins and, in the presence of an observer from Guinness World Records, made two timed runs in a Veyron Super Sport at an average of 268 miles per hour. The automotive world will never see its like again.

Bugatti Veyron 16.4	
Years of production	**2005–**
Engine	**8.0-liter quad-turbo DOHC W-16**
Output	**1,001 horsepower at 6,000 rpm**
Torque	**922 lb-ft (1,250 Nm) at 5,500 rpm**
Curb weight	**4,162 pounds (1,888 kg)**
0–62 mph/0–100 kph	**2.5 seconds**
Top speed	**252 miles per hour (406 kph)**
Number produced	**still in production**

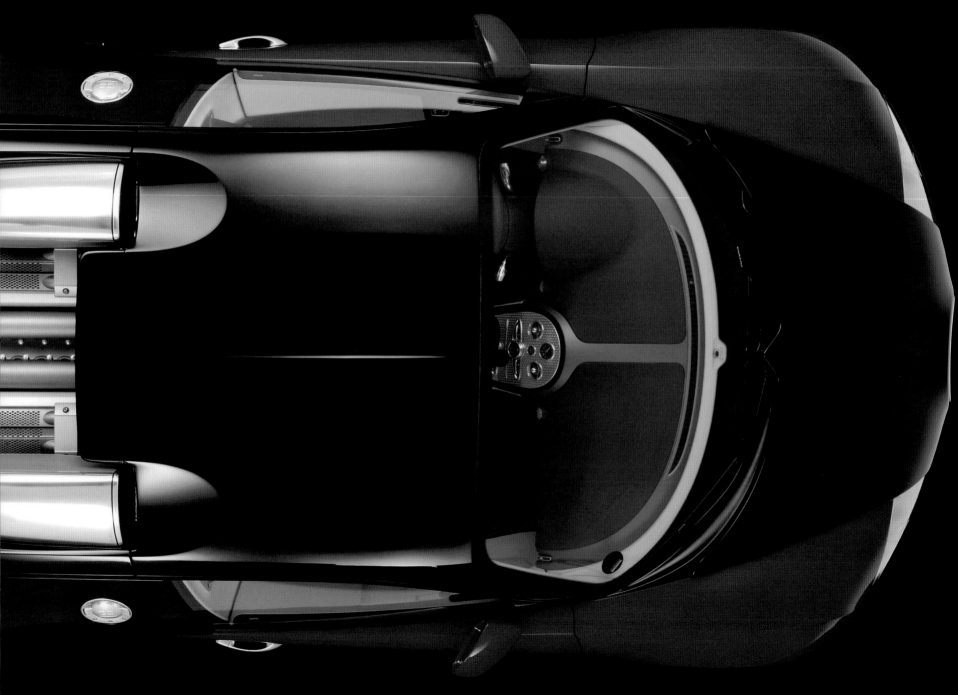

pagani
ZONDA F
roadster

Small-manufacturer supercars come and go—or rather, more often than not, they achieve the latter before the former, leaving behind nothing but a few concept models and a rapidly disseminating miasma of shattered dreams. Even those that actually arrive for public consumption are often regarded as mere curios; the products of Koenigsegg, for instance, are still viewed with a degree of detached bemusement (although this could be because of that company's dogged persistence in attempting to channel 1,000-plus horsepower to the road without the assistance of front driveshafts or space-age software).

Pagani, though, emerged with a healthy degree of credibility, thanks in part to founder Horacio Pagani's background in the heartland of supercars. The Argentine-born

Pagani worked at Lamborghini, engineering the run-out Countach anniversary model and creating a replacement for the Jalpa—which never saw the light of day owing to Lambo's fluctuating financial position. Striking out on his own, Pagani embarked on a project to create the ultimate supercar. And although you could argue that this is a well-trodden path, you only have to lift the enormous but deceptively light rear deck of the Zonda to see how Pagani got this car so exquisitely right: Nestled in the heart of an engine bay that is a beautiful piece of art in itself is a V-12 with the magical Mercedes-Benz star emblazoned on it. Here is a name to reassure, one that speaks of attention to detail and precise quality of assembly.

The first Zonda C12 of 1999 used the 389-horsepower Mercedes M120 6-liter V-12 engine—originally from the S600. In subsequent evolutions Pagani upgraded to a 7-liter AMG-tuned version of the engine, and then a 7.3-liter that made 547 horsepower at 5,900 rpm, which in combination with the Zonda's svelte 2,855-pound (1,295 kg) curb

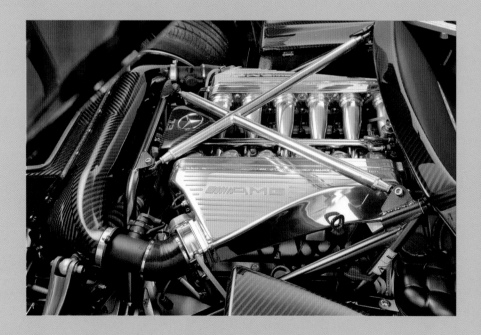

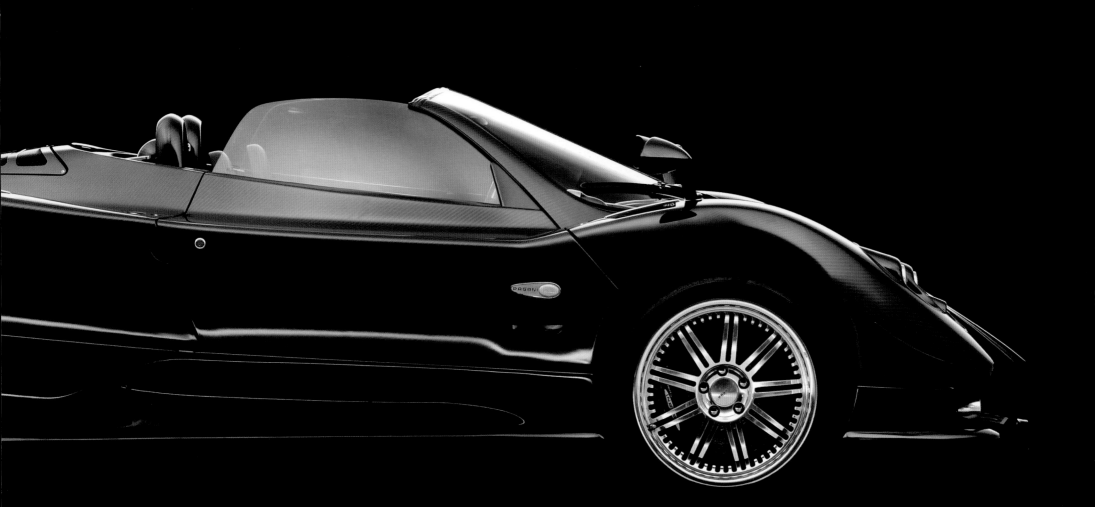

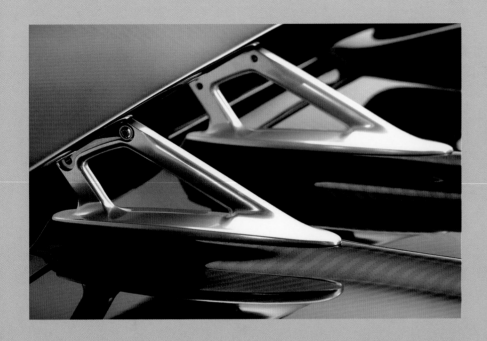

weight gave all the acceleration you would expect from 422 horsepower per metric ton. Pagani also worked on reducing all-up weight; the open-top Zonda F Roadster of 2006 pictured here (the F is for Pagani's idol, Argentine racing legend Juan Manuel Fangio) weighed no more than its coupe sibling thanks to minimal extra bracing. Pagani claimed 2,712 pounds (1,230 kg) for both cars and furnished an heroic 650 horsepower from the engine at 6,200 rpm. Power to weight? 529 horsepower per metric ton.

When the Zonda was first launched, only the venerable McLaren F1 was quicker. As detailed, in the intervening years Pagani has made his car lighter and considerably more powerful, culminating in the limited-run, 2,434-pound (1,104 kg) Zonda R (of which only 15 customer cars were made, plus one for the factory), which used the 5,987cc V-12 designed for the CLK GTR Le Mans car. With a dry sump and a throttle body for each cylinder, this one could spin to 8,000 rpm and peak at 739 horsepower on the way, thus achieving the standstill-to-62-mile-per-hour benchmark in a scarcely

Frank Stephenson

" This is kind of a take-off of a Group C racer but with a modern touch. There's a bit of the Enzo in there—it looks Italian to me. The quality of this car is amazing; I know Pagani pretty well and he gave me a tour of the factory. The attention to detail is outstanding. "

credible 3.0 seconds. For those with 1.4 million Euros burning a hole in their pockets during the worst global recession since the 1930s, it was a neat investment (snark if you will; Pagani had taken orders for 10 of the 15 Zonda Rs before the prototype was finished).

But the Zonda offers more than mere acceleration. Every aspect of its construction feels unique and delightfully tailored; you may cavil at the quilt-effect interior of the Roadster, but when you get up close you can see where the money is going. The Mercedes-Benz V-12 in the back is not just some bought-in piece of technology—it's totemic to the entire project. Pagani aspires to the finest levels of craftsmanship, and the steady flow of high net-worth individuals to the factory—based in Modena, of course, the heart of Supercar Valley—is a testament to the company's work. The cabin blends race car levels of preparation with fine hides and pleasingly machined aluminum. As a piece of art it would delight, even if it were never to move.

Frank Stephenson

"

When I look at it it looks more like a race car than a road car, with the shrunken surfaces and everything pulled in tight. The interior is where it goes away from that—the materials are really good, although maybe a bit flashy for some tastes, and you lose that sense of lightness.

"

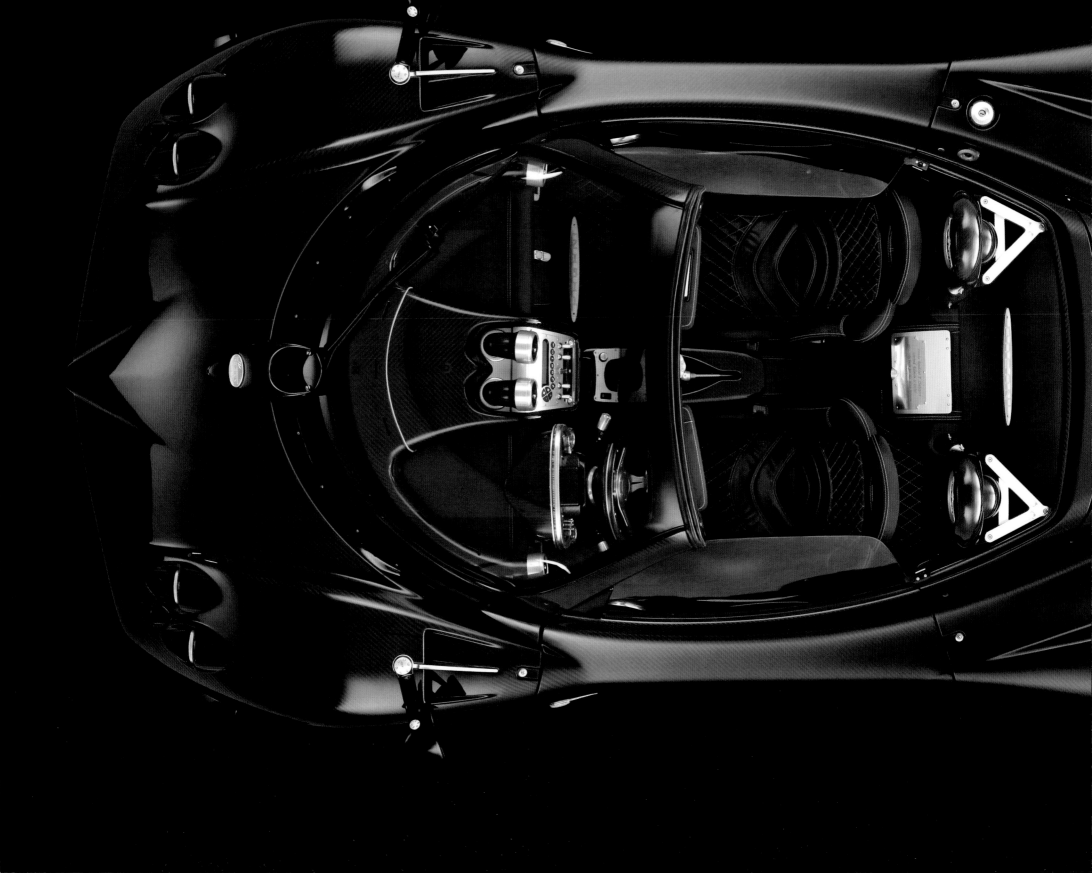

That may be quite a good thing, because there are few public roads in the world where one could unleash the full extent of the Zonda's performance without incurring the wrath of the local authorities, and even fewer racing circuits where one could explore its limits without running out of room. The internal combustion engine has come a long way since Karl Benz first putt-putted his way out of his workshop in his mechanical carriage, and the declining stock of fossil fuels means that we may soon have to embrace alternative means of propulsion.

In Benz's era, it was believed that the mechanical carriage was a strange and satanic device that would terrify horses and people in equal measure. To that end, the earliest drivers were often forced by law to employ a minion to run ahead of them with a red flag to warn sensitive souls of the motor car's imminent approach. Benz, perhaps, might take some solace in the fact that one of the ultimate expressions of the gasoline-powered car—and one that bears his surname on the engine cover—was still provoking the irk of twits, conservatives, and nincompoops over a century later.

Pagani Zonda F Roadster	
Year of production	**2006**
Engine	**7.3-liter Mercedes-Benz AMG 60-degree V-12; 48 valves**
Output	**650 horsepower at 6,200 rpm**
Torque	**575 lb-ft (780 Nm) at 4,050 rpm**
Curb weight	**2,712 pounds (1,230 kg)**
0–62 mph/0–100 kph	**3.6 seconds**
Top speed	**214 miles per hour (345 kph)**
Number produced	**25**

ferrari
599 GTB
fiorano

18

During Enzo Ferrari's dotage his eponymous company, under Fiat's ownership, broke with tradition and relocated the engine from its customary location between the driver and the front wheels to a more dynamically fashionable position just ahead of the rear wheels. After the Daytona was replaced in the 1970s, there would not be another mighty front-engined Ferrari berlinetta until the late 1990s.

The 550 Maranello restored the balance, putting the horse back in front of the cart and leaving nothing in that void behind the driver but a perfunctory luggage space and a fuel tank big enough for an adventurous pilot to pass from one extremity of a continent almost to its opposite. The car was a critical and commercial triumph. Its successor, the 575M, went calamitously wrong somewhere, and was panned by road testers and largely shunned by Ferrari's potential customers. Enzo may have long since departed the mortal firmament, but his firm responded in a manner of which he would have greatly approved: angrily dismissing the criticisms, clamping down even further on test models (so the flow of vehicles to the press went from "dead slow" to "stop"), while quietly producing a new model that would deliver the ultimate riposte to the 575M's critics. The 599 GTB, when it arrived in 2006, was new almost from the ground up, and it stunned road testers with its combination of explosive acceleration, cornering poise, and long-distance civility.

Where the 550M and 575M were based on the almost-antediluvian chassis construction of tubular steel, the 599's underpinnings were more complicated and costly. The chassis followed similar principles but was now made from lighter, stiffer aluminum, giving the 599 a claimed curb weight of 3,722 pounds (1,690 kg). It was therefore no lightweight still, but improvements elsewhere yielded a quantum leap

Frank Stephenson

"
This car looks great in the flesh. In photographs it seems to look much larger than it is. It's very taut. There's a lot of tension there, a feline quality. I love the side view of this car. And then when you walk round it you see the things that take weight out of it, such as the C-pillars and the massive intake at the front.
"

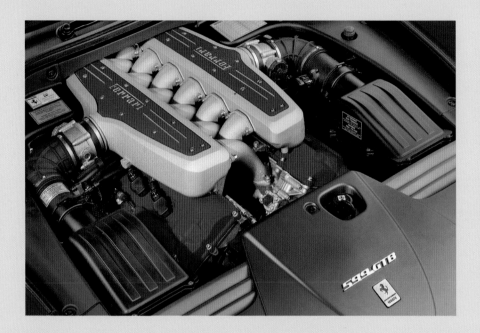

in performance over its predecessors. The fuel tank was located within the extended wheelbase to optimize the distribution of the mass, and the race-bred 5,999cc V-12 from the Enzo was re-engineered to suffuse it with manners befitting a grand tourer. Even so, peak output was 612 horsepower at 7,600 rpm and 448 lb-ft at 5,600 rpm, although given a long and straight enough road the musically inclined driver could spin the V-12 up to 8,400 rpm.

To emphasize what a step forward this car was from its predecessor, consider its power-to-weight ratio: 362 horsepower per metric ton compared with 291. The 599 was not even operating within the same ballpark. From a standing start it could hit 100 miles per hour in the same time that merely quick cars would take to reach the 62-mile-per-hour/100-kilometer-per-hour benchmark (which the 599 would have passed in 3.7 seconds).

Of course, no contemporary Ferrari would be complete without a smattering of Formula 1–derived technology, and the 599 benefited from access to the company's new wind tunnel, which overlooks the gate at the eastern end of the Maranello campus. The 599's optimized underbody enabled it to generate sufficient downforce at high speeds to go without exaggerated aerodynamic addenda. Its semi-automatic gearbox, operated in the F1 style via paddles on the steering wheel, changed gear in 100 milliseconds (and in true F1 style, by the time the first 599s were reaching customers, even this technology had been rendered obsolete by the latest seamless-shift systems).

The gearshift response times, along with the levels of traction and stability control intervention, were controlled via Manettino dials in the cockpit, much like those of the F1 cars of the time. These dials also modulated the responses of the magneto-rheological semi-active dampers—this time a technology not permitted in F1. Magnetic fields acted upon the damper liquid, changing its viscosity (and, therefore, the bump

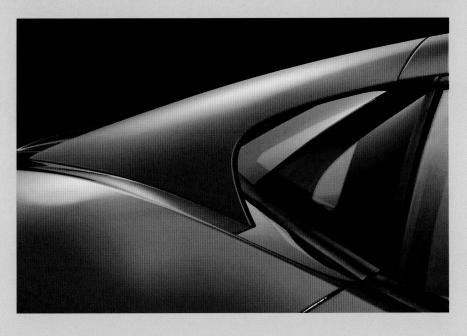

Frank Stephenson

"

It's actually asymmetrical—there are a couple of elements that are only on one side—and that makes it really feel designed for purpose. It works so well, all the lines run nicely together. It's really well defined. My only reservation is that I don't like cars to be bigger than they need to be; they tend to be out of proportion and have overhangs that are too long.

"

and rebound characteristics of the dampers) according to the driver's preference. It was a remarkably sophisticated setup, but it drew criticism from some quarters for being too coarsely grouped into a handful of broad-brush options, so that often one would find the desired damper settings accompanied by gearshift and traction parameters that were too aggressive, or too passive, but somehow never quite on the mark. Signor Ferrari would no doubt have tutted and observed that the more setup options one gives a driver, the more they are inclined to tinker—and the worse they make it for themselves.

There were other cars—indeed, other very rapid cars—competing for the patronage of the moneyed. But somehow none of them could combine that sheer pace with almost diplomatic civility, an exquisitely indulgent cabin, and a heady dose of Enzo charisma. With the 599, Ferrari not only re-established itself as the pre-eminent manufacturer of superior grand tourers, it also redefined the parameters of what a GT ought to be.

Ferrari 599 GTB Fiorano

Years of production	**2006–**
Engine	**6.0-liter DOHC V-12**
Output	**612 horsepower at 7,600 rpm**
Torque	**448 lb-ft (607 Nm) at 5,600 rpm**
Curb weight	**3,722 pounds (1,690 kg)**
0–62 mph/0–100 kph	**3.7 seconds**
Top speed	**over 205 miles per hour**
Number produced	**still in production**

ATOM 3

19

The Ariel Atom may have its roots in the sort of quirky backyard engineering project that is so quintessentially British, but its daringly minimalist concept could set the tone for future supercars as the world transitions away from fossil fuels. It began life in Coventry University's School of Transport Design in 1994 with a brief from senior lecturer Simon Saunders, an industry veteran, to sketch a putative two-seater sports car. The only constraints were that it should weigh no more than 500 kg (1,102 pounds) and cost no more than £10,000.

Enthused by some of the responses, Saunders then chose four pupils to work on the notional project; one of them, Nik Smart, would ultimately design what became the Ariel Atom. The Lightweight Sports Car, as it was then known, appeared as a non-running prototype at the British motor show in 1996, based around Ford components

(Ford actually provided a Fiesta free of charge as a donor car) and a chassis formed from raw materials furnished—along with a cash donation—by British Steel.

The idea of a spiritual successor to the Lotus Seven struck a chord with showgoers and the project gained momentum. Saunders found the necessary finance to form a company to usher the LSC through development and into production. Three years later, the newly founded Ariel Motor Company was ready to invite journalists to test drive the Atom.

Even with a modestly powered 1.8-liter Rover K-series engine mounted amidships, driving through a five-speed gearbox, the Atom 1 was fast and focused, and not especially forgiving when pushed to its limits—hardly surprising given its light weight and race-style suspension setup of wishbones and pushrod-actuated adjustable dampers. It demanded to be driven like a go-kart, thrown into corners and then corrected sharply when its tail stepped out; it appealed to the track day market, but sales were sluggish.

Frank Stephenson

"
This car brings you back to the beauty of technology. I love this kind of stuff. You can look at it as being like a fighter plane, minimalist and functional, or like an organism or animal where the skin is transparent and you can see the bone structure through it.
"

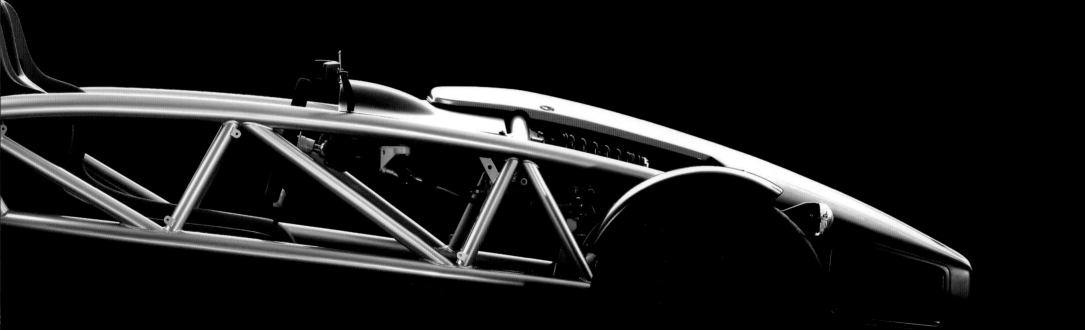

The 2003 Atom 2 was a slightly more civilized beast, and yet even more powerful thanks to the replacement of the aging Rover lump with Honda's musical 2-liter 160-horsepower VTEC engine. The six-speed transmission felt more race-like, and enterprising buyers could specify a supercharger option that brought the power up to 300 horses. If any of those enterprising drivers ever found themselves at a set of traffic lights next to a Bugatti Veyron, they could be assured that their Atom could keep pace with it until well beyond 100 miles per hour, after which the Veyron's less draggy bodyshell (not to mention its 1,001-horsepower engine) would enable it to pull clear. This process would not take as long as they might expect, however: The supercharged Atom can break the 100-mile-per-hour barrier in a little less than seven seconds.

At first glance the Atom 3 shown here, which arrived in 2007, seems little different. Look again: The latticework between the chassis rails runs in the opposite direction, yielding better cabin space. The engine mounts were revised to reduce the vibrations

Frank Stephenson

" It gives it a sense of lightness and it's also very functional. There's a real authenticity to this design. It's kind of like a Ducati motorbike, where you can see the trellis frame, and it has a dynamic movement all of its own. There's even a beauty in the welds. The simplicity of it attracts me. I don't know how you'd go about restyling it because it isn't really styled; you'd have to come up with a new chassis concept. "

that had bedeviled the first two models, and the engine itself was the latest Honda 2-liter VTEC, producing 245 horsepower in standard form and venting through twin exhaust pipes. Sensibly, Ariel capped the supercharged version (shown here) at 300 horsepower.

Despite its revised dampers, the Atom 3 is still a raw and uncompromising experience—and the limited-run Atom 500, launched in 2011, even more so. Powered by a bespoke flat-plane crank V-8, where each cylinder bank is based on the architecture of the engine from Suzuki's 200-mile-per-hour Hayabusa motorcycle, the Atom 500 still weighs just 1,213 pounds (550 kg) and requires the addition of a rear wing in order to put its 500 horsepower down on the road.

Although the market for a £150,000 car of this ilk is naturally limited—the standard car is more sensibly priced at around £35,000—as oil becomes more scarce it is natural that mainstream manufacturers will have to find ways to make their products go further on less fuel. So while the Ariel Atom is a particularly extreme example of the minimalist sports car, its abiding philosophy could become the template for all cars, not just performance machinery, in the decades to come.

Ariel Atom 3

Years of production	**2007–**
Engine	**2.0-liter supercharged Honda i-VTEC inline four, 16 valves**
Output	**300 horsepower at 8,200 rpm**
Torque	**210 lb-ft (284 Nm) at 6,100 rpm**
Curb weight	**1,350 pounds (612 kg)**
0–60 mph	**2.7 seconds**
Top speed	**155 miles per hour (250 kph)**
Number produced	**still in production**

alfa romeo
8C
competizione

To the average motorist in the early years of the twenty-first century, an Alfa Romeo supercar costing over $301,600 seemed a most bizarre proposition. When the 8C was unveiled at the 2006 Paris motor show, 55 years had elapsed since the brand was a dominant force in Formula 1 racing. In the interim, it had tumbled from prominence, been bought by the government to stave off bankruptcy, and settled into a comfortable pattern of producing mostly rather ordinary road cars, indifferently assembled and backed by insultingly poor customer service.

Still, one glance at the 8C gives a clue as to why enough well-heeled people signed the order book that Alfa could have sold the entire 500-unit production run more than twice over.

20

The car's appropriately descriptive name—"8C" for eight cylinders—harkens back to Alfa's pre-war glories. The original 8C was a supercharged straight-eight engine designed by Vittorio Jano—later the architect of the 1954 Lancia D50 Formula 1 racer before moving to Ferrari—and it propelled several Alfa road and racing cars during the 1930s. On the track, operated by Enzo Ferrari's eponymous team and boasting drivers of the caliber of Tazio Nuvolari, Alfa was unbeatable.

Back in the present, the Ferrari connection is just as strong, since both marques are part of the Fiat Group, as is Maserati. The twenty-first century 8C's engine is a racy flat-plane-cranked 4.7-liter V-8 with a peak output of 450 horsepower at 7,000 rpm; perhaps more significantly, it was designed and assembled in the Ferrari factory at Maranello.

The double-wishbone underpinnings were derived from the Maserati Quattro-porte, although the 8C's steel and carbon fiber chassis is shorter in the wheelbase. Alfa's engineers specified their own springs, dampers, and geometry, consciously

Frank Stephenson

"

This is a very sexy car from every angle. There's a simplicity and sensuality to it. The detailing is really fine. You look at it and nothing jolts you, there's nothing that doesn't make sense, there's no point where your eye stops and says, 'Well, where do I go now?'

"

went without Maserati's adaptive damping system, and tuned the car's handling at the Nürburgring as well as at Alfa's own test facilities. The car was some way removed from being a badge-engineered Maserati, although the production line was set up in Maserati's factory.

To keep weight down, much of the voluptuous skin was carbon fiber, but even so the 8C weighed in at 3,494 pounds (1,585 kg). Thanks to Alfa's decision to mount the six-speed semi-automatic gearbox just ahead of the rear axle, that weight was at least distributed evenly (51 percent front; 49 percent rear). The result was a handling balance predisposed to ultra-controllable oversteer drifts.

In truth, the 8C Competizione was a handful. Road testers at the time agreed that the chassis was rather too stiff, although it still demonstrated a tendency toward bounciness and body roll when cornering *in extremis*. But if the dynamics were not quite fully resolved, the 8C was still delightfully entertaining for the competent driver—

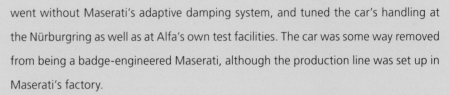

Frank Stephenson

"
The roof really gives this character. The A-pillars taper as they go down—I've never seen that done before, because it ought to look unstable, like a pyramid balancing on its tip. But they've pulled it off and it looks really cool. The one thing I don't like about it is the headlamp design. Not the shape, but the layout inside, with just a few lights of different sizes, as if it was the last thing they had in mind to do. They could have made it more beautiful.
"

especially with "Sport" mode activated, which altered the exhaust baffling for improved noise, sharpened the throttle response, quickened the gear shift, and set the traction control to "hands off."

In demeanor, then, this was a feisty beast better suited to short blasts around the track than to lengthy road trips. The interior, though, begged to differ: carbon fiber details, milled aluminum, and sumptuous stitched leather carried suggestions of grand touring.

Still, from the exquisite shape to the spine-tingling bark of the engine, this was a car to excite the senses. And if none of the privileged few to own one ever explored the outer edges of its performance envelope (with a top speed of 181 miles per hour and a claimed zero-to-60 sprint of 4.2 seconds, that's quite an extensive envelope), then all they would have to do is sit in the carbon-framed seat, prod the throttle, listen to the music of that engine, and have the wisdom of their purchase reaffirmed.

Alfa Romeo 8C Competizione

Years of production	**2007–2009**
Engine	**4.7-liter DOHC V-8, 32 valves**
Output	**450 horsepower at 7,000 rpm**
Torque	**354 lb-ft at 4,750 rpm**
Curb weight	**3,494 pounds (1,585 kg)**
0–60 mph	**4.2 seconds**
Top speed	**181 miles per hour (291 kph)**
Number produced	**500**

mclaren
MP4-12C

21

For a while, Formula 1 and its shifting network of allegiances stymied McLaren's development as a road car manufacturer. When the original F1 supercar was first mooted in the late 1980s, Honda was McLaren's race engine supplier—and indeed, Gordon Murray and his team evaluated the Honda NS-X and its engine before partnering with BMW. This alliance provided a consistent source of brand tension once McLaren signed a long-term Formula 1 engine deal with Mercedes-Benz from 1995 onward.

Neither the F1 nor the Mercedes-Benz SLR, built by McLaren from 2003 onward, sold in the numbers originally envisaged. This did not dissuade McLaren boss Ron Dennis from expanding the road car business, but he was determined to do it on his own terms: McLaren would build its own cars once again, rather than simply being a partner.

Frank Stephenson

"As you can see, we've got a blade on the side air intake where you wouldn't expect to find one. It's there for a purpose. The engineers didn't want the radiators at the front because you have to pass the fluid all the way through, it adds to the overall weight and it has an effect on the weight transfer under braking. So the usual thing to do would be to have the radiators at the back and facing into the wind to get maximum airflow. But if you turn them sideways the car can be a lot narrower, which is better. So how do you get the air to turn 90 degrees? Well, they calculated the curvature of that blade there so that the wind kind of sticks to it and then smacks the radiator really efficiently."

During the gestation of the MP4-12C, the relationship with Mercedes—including an equity holding—reached a largely amicable dissolution. In designing the new car, McLaren incorporated the lessons of the past and of the F1 in particular. The MP4-12C would be designed without compromise and mostly hand-built to McLaren's famous quality standards, but each car would take days rather than months to manufacture and would sell at the more accessible price point of $229,000.

To appreciate McLaren's ambitions for its automotive division—another four models are planned, with a maximum volume of 4,400 units a year—you have to visit its headquarters in Woking, England. But you'll have to look carefully. To sell cars in the numbers it hopes, it had to build a separate factory next to the existing McLaren Technology Centre—but to comply with stringent planning restrictions, the new McLaren Production Centre is barely visible from the road and adjacent parkland, even though its floor plan is big enough to accommodate three jumbo jets. All 180,000

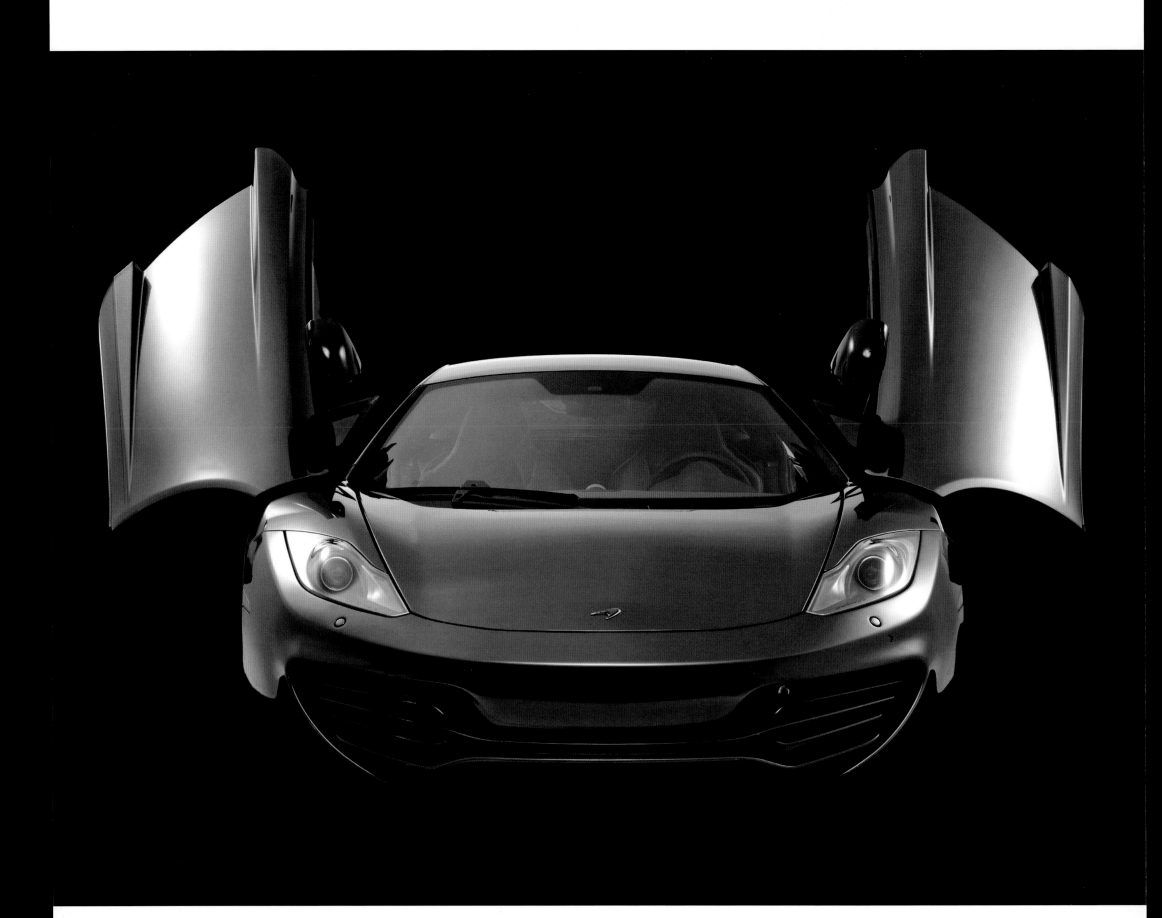

square meters of soil excavated during the build was retained on site—so as not to infuriate local residents with a constant procession of heavy traffic—and then reused to screen the building from view.

Having stepped back from the Formula 1 operation early in 2009, Dennis brought his legendary attention to detail to bear on the new facility, even insisting that its length and width were altered so that the (custom-specified) floor tiles would not have to be cut. Laugh if you will, but this shaved three weeks from the schedule, helped keep the project on budget, and saved a heap of waste going to landfill.

The key to McLaren's economies of scale is the remarkable "MonoCell," a one-piece carbon fiber structure akin to the central tub of a Formula 1 car. Other supercars have been built around carbon fiber monocoques, but not at this price—and, where an F1's monocoque took 3,000 hours of intricate laying up, when the new factory is on full song McLaren will be able to produce an MP4-12C MonoCell in four hours.

Frank Stephenson

"

The face is very expressive. When you have a sports car like this, with a couple of small radiators up front, they tend to have the same kind of openings so the headlights are an important way to give it character. The headlights were an area where we had complete freedom, so we put in some slots around the headlamp which are actually open by 1 mm and look like gills, then we have the daytime running lamps arranged in the shape of the McLaren 'speed mark'. Unlike, say, Audi LED running lamps which are very intense, we put caps in front of each LED so it softens the light. It bleeds into the gills and creates a halo.

"

Frank Stephenson

" We didn't want to make a car that screamed 'Versace' or 'look at me.' We wanted something more subtle. There are huge numbers of people who want that kind of look and I think it's the right one for McLaren. From a graphic point of view, there's nothing on that car that doesn't need to be there. You have to have reversing lights, fog lights, the high-level brake light, and so on; but on the MP4-12C these features are designed to be noticeable only when they're functioning; they're quite integrated into the overall design. The reflectors are tucked into the space between the diffuser and bumper, while the reverse and fog lamp are a single unit within the trailing edge of the diffuser, and when they activate they glow correspondingly white or red. "

It is perhaps unfortunate that McLaren is still a nascent brand in road car terms, for by most objective yardsticks the MP4-12C is superior to its closest rival, the Ferrari 458 Italia. But what the McLaren lacks in Latin magic it makes up for in compromise-free engineering: Even the heating and ventilation system is bespoke, because to have bought an off-the-shelf system would have entailed raising the scuttle, compromising visibility, and forced a lose-lose choice between offsetting the pedals or moving the seats outward, adding 2 inches to the car's width. And if the styling lacks flamboyance, that's because the shape was determined by the mechanical packaging and its aerodynamic requirements, then handed over to the designers to "dress." A Ferrari-style curved waist over the rear wheels, for instance, would have added weight and raised the center of gravity, neither of which would have made the MP4-12C go faster or handle more nimbly. Instead, the car stands apart from fashion, unashamedly allowing form to be dictated by function.

Mounting the radiators flat to the inside of the car enables the MP4-12C's signature feature, its aggressively scalloped twin air scoops; the feature also keeps overall width down and provides the driver with a more useful view to the rear than most supercars. The suspension is also distinctive, with interconnected hydraulic dampers that provide far more progressive anti-roll characteristics than mechanical anti-roll bars (which are, in effect, undamped lateral springs); the result is a remarkably comfortable ride.

Unsurprisingly, McLaren dipped into its Formula 1 toolbox while tuning the chassis, finessing the MP4-12C's handling on its in-house simulator. The braking system incorporates a technology McLaren pioneered in Formula 1 in the late 1990s, before other teams clamored for it to be banned: selectively braking one or both of the rear wheels to improve cornering stability. In the MP4-12C, brake-steer is electronically adjudicated, whereas in Formula 1 the driver had to actuate it via a third pedal.

Although the MP4-12C is 200 kg (441 pounds) heavier than the F1 and its bespoke twin-turbo engine 35 horsepower less potent, the difference in acceleration between the two is best measured on the stopwatch rather than by the seat of the pants. The 12C covers the European-benchmark zero to 62 miles per hour in 3.3 seconds—3.1 seconds if wearing the track-oriented Pirelli rubber that's available as an option—while its flat plane–cranked V-8 emits a delicious bark up to the 8,500 rpm cut-off. The 443 lbs-ft (601 Nm) of torque from 3,000 to 7,000 rpm means that instant and devastating thrust is available in practically any gear, at any speed. Retardation is assisted by an integrated rear spoiler that pops up to act as an air brake.

Perhaps most remarkably of all—though unlikely to swing a purchasing decision—the MP4-12C emits 279g/km of CO_2. That means its engine makes each horsepower more carbon-efficiently than a Toyota Prius. Those of you reading this will no doubt have a clear opinion of which car you would prefer to drive. . . .

Frank Stephenson

" The exhaust pipes are where they are because of the downforce we wanted to generate. If you put the pipes where they usually go, the airflow isn't as clean, so by putting them up there we got the optimum airflow for downforce, plus that's the shortest route for the exhausts to come out so it saves weight. "

McLaren MP4-12C

Years of production	**2011–**
Engine	**3.8-liter twin-turbocharged V-8**
Output	**592 horsepower at 8,500 rpm**
Torque	**443 lb-ft (601 Nm) of torque at 3,000 to 7,000 rpm**
Curb weight	**3,200 pounds (1,451 kg) (est.)**
0–62 mph/0–100 kph	**3.3 seconds**
Top speed	**205 miles per hour (330 kph)**
Number produced	**in production**

Acknowledgments

Typing the words is only part of the journey in creating a book such as this. I'd like to thank everyone who played a part: James Mann for his energy, speed, and ability to get hold of extraordinarily rare cars (and for convincing their owners to lend them to us); Kevin Wood at the LAT Archive for reserving the Jim Clark mug; Mark Harrison, Dan Connell, and Gemma Petrillo at McLaren for allowing us to photograph an MP4-12C before production had even started; Frank Stephenson for giving generously of his time to cast an expert eye over our collection; and of course, the person without whom you would not be holding this book at all, its all-seeing editor, Jeffrey Zuehlke. Thanks also to my wife, Julie, for her love and support, and to the cats for not accidentally deleting anything.

—Stuart Codling

The idea for this book came up after the first title in this series, *Art of the Formula 1 Race Car* proved a great success. Early on, however, I wondered if we might get the same generous assistance from the supercar crowd that we had so richly enjoyed from the F1 fraternity. I shouldn't have worried, though, and was greatly relieved when longtime friend David Cottingham at DK Engineering agreed to help. His sons, James and Jeremy, supplied the F40, F50, 599, and Porsche Carrera GT from their fabulous showroom and put me in touch with owner Ian Tandy, who helped with the Ferrari Daytona and Lamborghini Miura. They also transported the cars to and from the studio. From then on it was easier, as it often is with these projects: Once you get a few "in the bag," the others begin to fall into place. So I am grateful to all those listed below who lent their cars, assisted in the studio, and drove transporters.

Thanks also go to Motorbooks, for whom I have photographed many books, and especially to editor Jeffrey Zuehlke, whose support never faltered. I am also always grateful to my family, who put up with me through this book after I said the last studio book would be the last; they know me better than that now!

The Cars

Ferrari F40, F50, 599, and Porsche Carrera GT . . . . DK Engineering
Lamborghini Miura and Ferrari Daytona . . . . Ian Tandy
Ferrari 275GTB/4 and Aston Martin DB4GTZ . . . . William Loughran
McLaren MP4-12C . . . . McLaren Automotive Ltd
Jaguar XJ220 . . . . Don Law
McLaren F1 . . . . Clive Joy
Maserati MC12 and Bizzarrini 5300 GT Strada . . . . .Autofocusimages
Alfa Romeo 33 Stradale . . . . Clive Joy
Lancia Stratos . . . . Fiskens
BMW M1 . . . . BMW UK
Alfa Romeo 8C . . . . .Alfa Romeo UK and Mitch Millett of Bauer Millett Alfa Romeo
Bugatti Veyron. . . . . .Romans International
Ariel Atom. . . . . Simon Saunders at the Ariel Motor Company
Mercedes 300SL. Chris Routledge at Coys
Pagani Zonda F Roadster. . . . . SuperVettura

The Studios

Plough Studios
Junction Eleven
John Colley Studios

Thanks also to

Anna Angelini at Alfa Romeo
Tommy Wareham at SuperVettura
Michael Lorusso at Romans International
Juliette Loughran at William Loughran

Mark Donaldson
James Mitchell at Fiskens
Martin Harrison at BMW
Alistair and Killian at Konig cars

Studio assistants: Jonathan Topps, Mark Brown, and Phil Mills

And the many others, too numerous to mention, who helped to transport the cars and put the book together. Thank you!

—James Mann

On the front cover: The McLaren F1

On the back cover: The Ferrari 275GTB/4

On the frontis: The Alfa Romeo 33 Stradale

On the title pages: The Lamborghini Miura

First published in 2011 by Motorbooks, an imprint of Quarto Publishing Group USA Inc., 400 First Avenue North, Suite 400, Minneapolis, MN 55401 USA

Motorbooks titles are also available at discounts in bulk quantity for industrial or sales-promotional use. For details write to Special Sales Manager at Quarto Publishing Group USA Inc., 400 First Avenue North, Suite 400, Minneapolis, MN 55401 USA.

To find out more about our books, visit us online at www.motorbooks.com.

Library of Congress Cataloging-in-Publication Data

Codling, Stuart, 1972-
Form follows function : the art of the supercar / text, Stuart Codling ; photographs, James Mann.
    p. cm.
Includes index.
ISBN 978-0-7603-4116-2 (hardbound with jacket)
1. Sports cars—Pictorial works. 2. Automobiles, Racing—Pictorial works. I. Mann, James, 1963– II. Title.
III. Title: Art of the supercar.
TL236.C535 2011
629.222'1—dc23
                                                                                    2011023797

Editor: Jeffrey Zuehlke
Design Manager: Kou Lor
Designer: Simon Larkin
Production Manager: Hollie Kilroy

Printed in China

10 9 8 7 6 5 4 3 2

Index

Alfa Romeo 8C Competizione, 202–211
Alfa Romeo 33 Stradale, 60–69
Alfieri, Giulio, 158
Ariel Atom, 8, 194–201
Aston Martin DB4GT Zagato, 20–29

Benz, Karl, 183
Bizzarrini, Giotto, 31, 33, 34, 49
Bizzarrini 5300GT Strada, 30–37
BMW M1, 90–99
Bugatti, Ettore, 165
Bugatti Veyron 16.4, 165–173

Carrera Panamericana, 146
Chiti, Carlo, 33, 61, 62, 65
Clarkson, Jeremy, 150

Dallara, Giampaolo, 49, 53, 82, 143
Dennis, Ron, 98, 123, 213
Dermott, Harold, 124
De Tomaso, Alejandro, 158

Fangio, Juan Manuel, 13, 179
Ferrari, Enzo, 49, 75, 108
Ferrari F40, 100–111
Ferrari F50, 134–143
Ferrari 250GTO, 25
Ferrari 275GTB/4, 38–47
Ferrari 365GTB/4 "Daytona," 70–79
Ferrari 599 GTB Fiorano, 184–193
Fiorio, Cesare, 82

Fitch, John, 18, 36
Frankel, Andrew, 108

Gandini, Marcello, 54, 81, 166
Giugiaro, Giorgetto, 54, 156

Jaguar XJ220, 112–121

Lamborghini, Ferruccio, 49
Lamborghini Miura, 48–59
Lancia Stratos, 8, 80–89

Maserati brothers (Alfieri, Bindo, Ernesto, Ettore), 155
Maserati MC12, 154–163
McLaren, Bruce, 123
McLaren F1, 6, 108, 122–133
McLaren MP4-12C, 9, 212–221
Mercedes-Benz 300S "Gullwing," 8, 10–19
Michelotto, 143
Murray, Gordon, 6, 123–124, 127, 213

Neerpasch, Jochen, 92, 96

Orsi, Alberto, 155, 156

Pagani, Horacio, 175
Pagani Zonda F Roadster, 9, 174–183
Parkes, Michael, 40, 82
Piëch, Ferdinand, 146, 169
Porsche Carrera GT, 144–153
Procar Series, 98

Raphanel, Pierre-Henri, 172
Reitzle, Wolfgang, 50
Rendle, Steve, 124
Rivolta, Renzo, 34

Saunders, Simon, 195–196
Scaglione, Franco, 65
Smart, Nik, 195
Stanzini, Paolo, 53
Stephenson, Frank, 7–9, 13, 14, 22, 26, 33, 34, 40, 42, 44, 50, 54, 57, 62, 72, 75, 82, 85, 86, 92, 95, 96, 102, 104, 107, 114, 118, 124, 127, 129, 130, 136, 139, 140, 149, 150, 158, 160, 162, 166, 168, 170, 179, 180, 186, 191, 196, 199, 204, 209, 214, 217, 218, 221
Stevens, Peter, 124, 127

Tavoni, Romolo, 33

Uhlenhaut, Rudolf, 11, 14

Veyron, Pierre, 166, 170

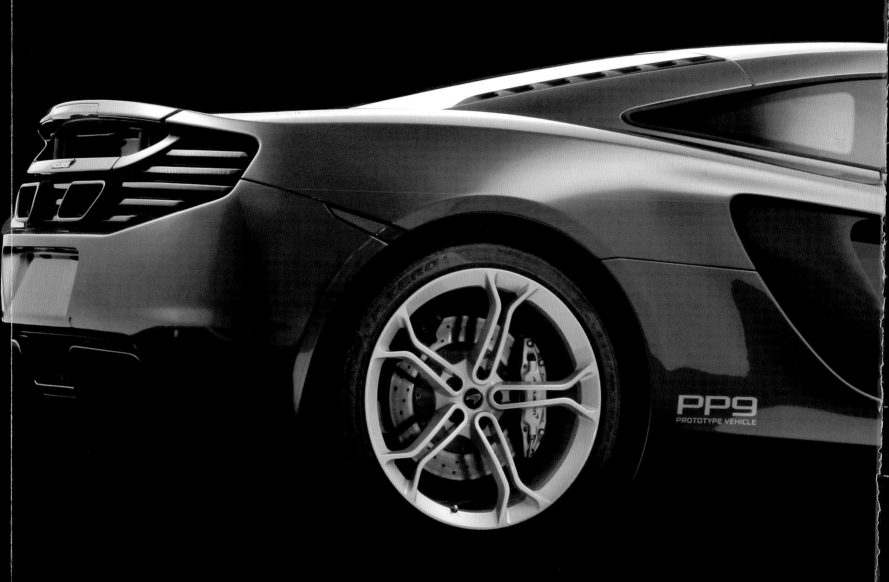